Choosing Small Trees

Choosing Small Trees

Peter McHoy

Published in the United States by
Laurel Glen Publishing
5880 Oberlin Drive, Suite 400
San Diego, CA 92121-4794
http://www.advmkt.com

Published in Great Britain by
Hamlyn, an imprint of
Octopus Publishing Group Ltd
2-4 Heron Quays
London E14 4JP

ISBN 1-57145-647-3
Library of Congress CIP data available upon request.

1 2 3 4 5 00 01 02 03 04
Produced by Toppan
Printed in China

Publishing Director
Alison Goff

Creative Director
Keith Martin

Executive Editor
Julian Brown

Editor
Karen O'Grady

Production
Sarah Scanlan

Picture Research
Liz Fowler

Senior Designer
Leigh Jones

Design
Birgit Eggers

N. American Edition
Publisher
Allen Orso

Managing Editor
JoAnn Padgett

Project Editor
Elizabeth McNulty

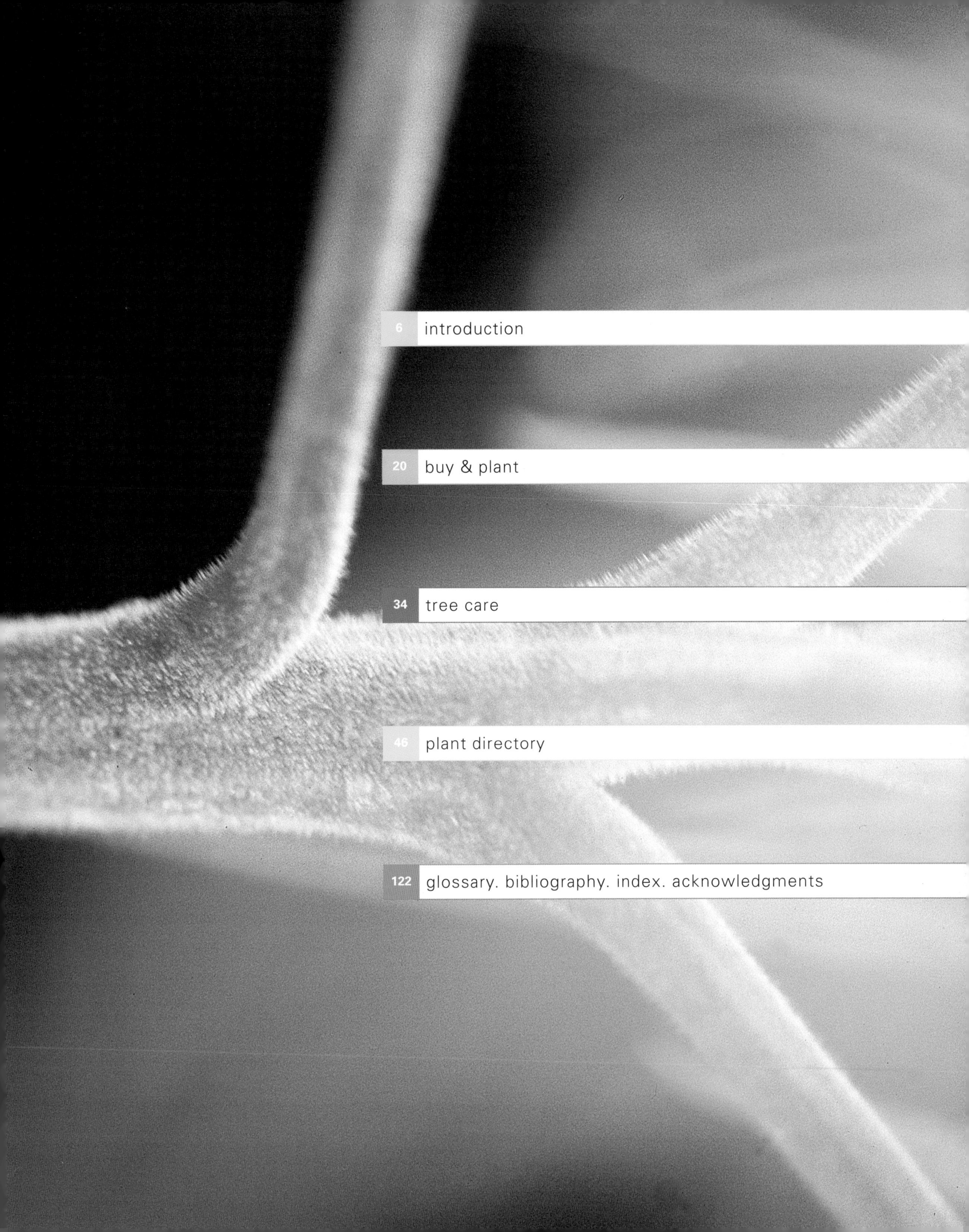

introduction

Small gardens need trees just as much as larger plots: the **right tree** can actually make a garden look bigger by encouraging you to look upward to the vertical space above; they can also mask the confines of the plot.

A small tree is a **better addition** to a small garden than a large shrub. The single trunk of a tree allows more scope for underplanting than a thicket of shrub stems, and there is less need to curb the spread along the ground.

We hope you'll be inspired by this book to plant plenty of trees if your garden lacks that vital vertical element at the moment. If you already have these important backbone plants in your garden, you'll find plenty of **hints and tips** in the following pages to make the most of them.

Trees vary in **size and shape** depending on their species, but this can be manipulated by the way they are grown. While most trees have a natural shape which is either spreading, upright, or weeping, many can be trained into forms that take up less space. For example, a standard tree has a clear trunk to a height of about 6 ft. (1.8 m) before the branches form a head at the top. A half-standard has a clear trunk of about 3 ft. (1 m) before the branches form a head. In time, you will have the **satisfaction** of watching your chosen trees grow and mature and make their lasting contribution to the beauty of your garden.

the role of garden trees

The structure of a tree has such a physical presence that one or more trees, carefully positioned, could make the main contribution to the look and atmosphere of your garden. As the dominant plant, it will influence the microclimate beneath and around it (making the soil drier and the site more shady), thus affecting the growth of the surrounding smaller plants.

Below are some examples of the role trees can play in small gardens. In any given situation, a tree can perform more than one function—screening eyesores and providing shade, for example.

As focal points

One of the tricks when designing a small garden is to make it appear bigger than it really is by drawing the viewer's eye to certain areas. This is done by creating a long view, or an illusion of one, using a path, low hedging, or steps with something at the end for the eye to settle on. The focal point at the end of the view could be a statue, seat, or fancy container, but a tree offers a natural yet long-lived focal point. The tree needs to be distinctive from a distance—a strong shape like an exclamation mark or a weeping standard. A bright foliage color works well too, so consider yellow or blue-green conifers.

As specimens

Like a tree used as a focal point, a specimen has to be distinctive and capable of holding the viewer's attention on its own, but, in this case, it can be viewed from any angle and not necessarily from a distance. A single tree in a small garden may look good planted in a lawn, which may be the only space where it can develop without encroaching on neighboring plants. For such a position, choose a subject with a feature that looks best in isolation, such as winter bark, and one that does not cast too much shade over the grass.

In mixed borders

Trees add height and a sense of maturity to mixed borders, and together with shrubs they form a backbone. As well as looking for a contrast of shape and foliage from among the chosen woody plants, their size should be in scale with the depth of the border. Aim to include both deciduous and evergreen woody subjects; two-thirds deciduous to one-third evergreen works well. Evergreens contribute winter interest and make a good foil for flowers, whereas deciduous trees let enough light through in spring to allow for carpets of spring-flowering bulbs.

Other subjects that work well in mixed borders are those that only cast a light shade and those with more than one feature of interest. Whenever possible, choose and position the trees and main shrubs first, then fill in the gaps with short-lived plants.

Right: *Prunus* x *sub-hirtella* 'Autumnalis' produces its semi-double white flowers intermittently all winter and has the bonus of good autumn foliage color.

Left: Golden conifers are especially useful during the winter months but contribute to the summer scene too. This one harmonizes with the *Catalpa bignnonioides* 'Aurea' behind.

Below: Many conifers have interesting textures and colors, making them useful for combination planting. Dwarf conifers are particularly useful.

As screens

Small gardens often entail a lack of privacy from neighbors; also eyesores such as garden sheds or oil tanks are all too obvious. Rather than simply stick a tree in front of the problem, experiment with placing a smaller specimen between you and the object to be screened. You can either do this in situ by getting a friend to hold canes of various sizes at different positions in the garden or by making a simple scale model of the garden with a viewing frame and use models of trees of different shapes and sizes.

As wildlife havens

Being longer lived and bigger, trees support a much wider range of wildlife than, for example, the same area of garden given over to bedding plants or perennials. Birds and countless insects can use them as a refuge. Native trees are often considered to be preferable by purists, and of these the ones most suitable for the smaller North American garden include the silver birch (*Betula pendula*) and holly (*Ilex aquifolium*), but any tree with blossom and fruits will attract insects and birds.

planning for year-round interest

As trees are long-term plants they will offer seasonal interest for many years, so it is worth considering them first when planning planting schemes for year-round color. Apart from the shape and form of the tree (*considered on pages 14–15*), the key seasonal features that a tree could add to the garden are: foliage, flowers, berries, and attractive bark.

Foliage

An evergreen will offer foliage all year round, although it will be appreciated most in winter and early spring when there is little else in leaf. Decid-uous trees are in leaf from spring to autumn, and the color might change throughout these sea-sons—some species are noted for their brilliant autumn tints. Aim for a balance of evergreen and deciduous woody subjects—too many evergreens make for a static and somber garden.

Flowers are impressive for a short while but a tree with attractive foliage will give a longer period of interest. Apart from the many shades of green, some species offer golden-yellow foliage (*Catalpa bignonioides* 'Aurea,' for example); red/ purple foliage (such as *Fagus sylvatica* 'Purpurea Pendula'); silver/gray foliage (*Pyrus salicifolia* 'Pendula'); and variegated foliage (many varieties of English holly *Ilex aquifolium*). Most useful for a small garden are pale colors like gray/silver, blue-green, or paler greens—if these are positioned at the far end, they will make the garden seem longer.

Flowers

Most trees with spectacular blooms tend to produce them either in spring or in summer. Trees like the

Prunus incisa is a lovely flowering cherry for spring, and the variety 'Prae-cox' (illustrated) will even bloom in winter.

Japanese cherries, magnolias, and laburnum look stunning when in full flower, but offer little for the rest of the year, so take this into account when planning year-round color. By all means use them as seasonal highlights but combine them with colorful evergreens or plants with more than one season of interest.

Spring

Catkins are an early herald of spring and these can be provided in a small garden by choosing *Salix caprea* 'Pendula,' a small umbrella-like tree with silvery catkins and gold anthers. Young foliage on many deciduous trees can also provide fresh color as the leaves unfold.

There are a great many spring-flowering trees to choose from, so remember to be selective: a small garden will probably need no more than two or three. The Japanese cherry trees are well-known for their spring blossom. *Prunus* 'Amanogawa' has fragrant, semidouble shell-pink flowers, *P.* 'Kanzan' has deep pink buds that open to fully double rich pink flowers, while the cascading *P.* 'Kiku-shidare-zakura' has pink buds and fully double rose pink flowers.

Late spring is the time for *Amelanchier lamarckii* to become covered in clouds of starry white flowers. One of the earliest flowering crab apples is *Malus floribunda* with its deep pink buds opening to pale pink, then white flowers. Magnolias like *Magnolia soulangeana* always impress with their primitive tulip-like flowers on the leafless branches. Choose a named variety so the tree will flower when young.

Other possibilities include the white, pink, or red flowers of *Crataegus* (hawthorn) species and hybrids; the yellow pea flowers of the pea tree (*Caragana arborescens*) and the Judas tree (*Cercis siliquastrum*) with clusters of rose-lilac flowers around its branches.

The yellow flowers of *Laburnum* x *watereri* appear as late spring becomes summer, the drooping racemes making an impressive show (but note that all parts of the plant are poisonous).

Summer

There are fewer trees that flower in summer; many are large shrubs and need specific site conditions. For impressive flowers in early to mid-summer, consider *Cornus kousa* with its numerous white flowers (strictly speaking these are bracts) which makes a stunning specimen given the right site.

Later in the summer *Eucryphia* x *nymansensis* is covered with beautiful single white flowers set off by showy yellow stamens.

For golden-yellow foliage all through the summer *Robinia pseudoacacia* 'Frisia' takes some beating and has become a popular choice in many gardens.

A

Prunus x yedoenisis 'Shidare-yoshino' (sometimes found with the name *P.* 'Yoshina Pendula') has branches that sometimes weep to the ground.

B

Prunus 'Taihaku' (you will sometimes find it written 'Tai Haku') makes a fairly large tree, but it's a spectacular flowering cherry.

C

Prunus 'Shogetsu' is a small tree with double white flowers that contrast well with the coppery young leaves.

D

Robinia psuedoacacia 'Frisia' retains a fresh-looking golden color throughout the summer months.

Autumn

For late-season interest, some trees offer brilliant autumn tints that almost set the sky alight, others offer displays of fruits. Such seasonal highlights will not necessarily put on a dazzling display every year as they are weather dependent. Some years strong winds strip the leaves off the trees while they are looking their most colorful. When the weather turns harsh early, birds may strip trees of berries almost overnight. If possible, choose a tree that offers more than just berries or autumn color.

The best autumn leaf color is usually seen where trees are growing on poor soils such as thin chalky or sandy soils, but there are exceptions such as *Cornus kousa*, so check the details in the Plant Directory. Even with the same species some varieties have a reputation for producing better color than others. *Acer griseum* has a reliable autumn color. Another good one is *Malus tschonoskii* with leaves of yellow, orange, purple, and scarlet. The staghorn sumac (*Rhus typhina*) has large pinnate leaves which are brightly colored in autumn and there may also be hairy cone-shaped autumn fruits.

Fruits are often thought of as an autumn feature although those of the cherries (*Prunus*) actually ripen in the summer. Fruits add color and provide a natural source of food for birds, but can be a nuisance when they fall on hard landscaping or paths, so consider the site carefully. *Malus* 'John Downie' is one of the best of the fruiting crabapples with its large yellow and red fruits. The small rowan *Sorbus vilmorinii* offers an attractive autumn combination of bronze-red foliage and loose clusters of berries that change from red to pinkish-white. For color from autumn through until winter, consider

Acer Palmatum 'Osakazuki' is one of many fine Japanese maples. These trees are often shrub-like while young.

Arbutus x *andrachnoides* has wonderful cinnamon-colored bark that simply demands your attention. The tree can eventually grow too large for a very small garden, however.

Cotoneaster 'Hybridus Pendulus' with its long-lasting red berries and glossy evergreen foliage; or *Crataegus prunifolia* for its rich autumn color and persistent fruit.

Winter

Conifers come into their own in winter with their evergreen foliage in various colors, and look especially effective combined with ornamental grasses or with winter- or spring-flowering heathers for extra interest. The Irish yew (*Taxus baccata* 'Fastigiata') is grown for its easy-to-keep-neat column shape. Use it on its own as a focal point, or plant in rows for a formal effect.

Tree bark becomes a feature in winter when the distraction of leaves and flowers has gone. It is set off to best advantage by a solid background such as a conifer hedge, lawn, or planting of evergreen perennials. Silver birch (*Betula pendula*) is well known for its graceful habit and white stems, but for further winter color, underplant it with a carpet of evergreen perennials and early spring bulbs. Although the species itself is likely to grow too tall for a small garden, the variety 'Youngii' is very suitable, and in winter the pendulous branches will be bare and expose the trunk that's screened in summer.

The paperbark maple (*Acer griseum*) will, in time, develop a peeling bark that is brown with orange beneath, and it has the bonus of good autumn color. *A. davidii* has a green and white striped bark as its main feature but also offers autumn foliage and fruits. The peeling bark of *Prunus serrula* is a polished red-brown, a warming sight on a cold winter day.

Finally, for the sheer delight of seeing flowers in the middle of winter why not consider *Prunus* x *subhirtella*. The white flowers are borne through the winter, and it also offers good autumn foliage.

Triple-interest trees

Amelanchier lamarckii has spring blossom among copper-tinted leafy shoots, black berries, and brilliant red and orange autumn color.

Arbutus unedo is a small evergreen tree that grows in beauty as it matures when the bark becomes deep brown and shredded. The white flowers and strawberry-like fruits are borne at the same time in late autumn.

the question of size

The importance of choosing a tree that is a suitable size for the site has already been stressed. Tree size, for the purposes of gardening, is expressed as the height and spread in feet or meters, but it's impossible to be precise. Much depends on the variety chosen, how it is trained, and on the environment it found itself in through its life. Such factors as the soil type and depth, aspect and local weather conditions all play their part. For example, trees tend to grow taller in sheltered, lightly shaded positions than they do in open positions exposed to winds.

Despite the precision with which measurements are often quoted in reference books, there is a certain amount of leeway to tree dimensions. Height and spreads are often given at set periods such as five or ten years after planting or expressed as ultimate heights—the latter can be unnecessarily off-putting as some trees are very slow-growing yet long-lived. In the Plant Directory we've given the likely height in a garden setting after about 20 years. A few may continue to grow beyond the height suggested, but only very slowly. We have also placed the trees in broad steps of about 5 ft. (1.5 m), as more precise measurements are meaningless with so many variables to affect growth.

The speed of growth and the shape of the tree is also relevant to whether it is suitable for the space allocated to it. This can be best be illustrated by the following examples.

Trees that remain small

The following trees are examples of those that remain a fixed height as they have been grafted on to stems of a fixed height. Any growth will take place in the weeping branches which can be easily trimmed back if need be.

COTONEASTER
'Hybridus Pendulus' is actually a spreading bush that has been grafted on top of a stem of an upright species such as *C. bullatus* to given the appearance of a small weeping tree.

PRUNUS
'Kiku-shidare-zakura' is a weeping cherry that has been grafted on to a stem of *P. avium*.

CARAGANA ARBORESCENS
'Pendula' is grafted on to the top of a straight stem to form a small weeping tree.

SALIX CAPREA
'Kilmarnock' ('Pendula') reaches only 6–10 ft. (2–3m) depending on the height of its grafting stem.

Malus x *purperea* 'Lemoinei,' which is sometimes seen simply as *Malus* x *lemoinei*, is one of many small-flowering crabs. This one is grown mainly for its colorful foliage.

Juniperus communis 'Hibernica,' the Irish juniper, is a good choice when you need a space-saving conifer. It proves especially useful for formal gardens that need an upright punctuation point.

Larger but slow-growing

ARBUTUS UNEDO
is slow-growing for about the first 15 years, so do not be put off by an ultimate height of 15 ft. (4.5 m).

FLOWERING CRABS (MALUS HYBRIDS)
the height depends on the choice of rootstock; if they are available on a dwarfing apple rootstock, such as M27, they will remain very small.

HOLLIES
are slow-growing so don't be put off by ultimate height. *Ilex aquifolium* can be grown as a mop-head standard.

There is also the aptly-named 'Green Pillar,' an erect form with a narrow growth habit.

Tall but narrow

In a small garden it is the horizontal space that is at such a premium so trees that are tall but have a narrow growth habit are particularly useful.

JUNIPERUS SCOPULORUM 'SKYROCKET'
The most extreme example and the narrowest of all conifers. An example taken at the Hillier Garden and Arboretum in Hampshire, England, shows a 16 ft. (5 m) high specimen having a diameter of only 1 ft. (30 cm).

PRUNUS 'AMANOGAWA'
Other examples include *Prunus* 'Amanogawa' a small columnar tree with erect branches.

ULMUS 'WREDEI AUREA'
An unusual elm, *Ulmus* x *hollandica* 'Wredei' (syn. *U. minor* 'Dampieri Aurea') makes a tight golden pillar that may have a spread of only 2 ft. (75 cm) by the time it's 10 ft. (3 m) tall.

practical considerations

As trees are a long-term feature of a garden, you want to able to reap the benefit of them as they mature rather than have to hack back or even remove them when they are in their prime simply because of a lack of foresight at the time of planting. The following headings cover the main practical points to consider. Taken together it sounds rather off-putting, so it is worth pointing out that one of the best places to plant a tree in small garden is to one side of the lawn, with at least 3 ft. (1 m) diameter of turf removed for ease of maintenance. Small trees can also work well in borders or near water if the pond is netted in autumn to stop the leaves falling in.

Planting near boundaries

Avoid planting trees where the branches will overhang your neighbor's garden or the highway. In most areas, your neighbor has the right to remove any overhanging branches, which could spoil the shape of your tree as well as cause upsets between you. The local authorities may also contact you if overhanging vegetation is blocking road visibility.

Planting near hard landscaping

Leaves, fallen fruits, and the like cause little problem when they drop onto a lawn or border soil as earthworms break down the leaves into the soil and fruits soon rot away. However, where the ground has hard landscaping such as a patio, rocks and stones, path, driveway, or steps, such fallout can be at best a nuisance or at worst dangerous when wet. Avoid planting a tree near where you park your car, particularly if it has fruit, as the bird mess and staining can damage paintwork.

Tree roots can cause damage to paths and driveways. There is also the risk that weed-killers used on these areas could run off down to the tree roots and cause damage.

Prickly trees such as hawthorn (*Crataegus*) or holly (*Ilex*) can be a nuisance near a narrow but well-used path.

Planting near buildings

There is nothing to be gained by planting a tree near a building. Foundations can be weakened by tree roots, which can also effect drains, sewers, and water supplies. Above ground, the tree will reduce the amount of light reaching the inside of the building. Routine maintenance such as dealing with blocked gutters or painting will all be made much harder if a tree is in the way.

Insurance companies are much more aware about the dangers of trees near buildings these days, although most serious damage is restricted to species not mentioned in this book such a weeping willows and poplars. The problem is also aggravated by soil type, with tree roots in clay soils causing the most concern.

Acer palmatum dissectum is generally a bit shrubby in habit, plants tend to be mushroom-shaped when young. You can rely on a good display of autumn color before the leaves fall.

Sorbus aucuparia is grown mainly for its great display of bright red berries. Unfortunately birds also find these very attractive and often the trees can be stripped prematurely.

From the tree's point of view a building is not the ideal neighbor. The soil near the building foundations is likely to be poor and full of rubble. The tree will almost certainly develop a lop-sided shape as it will be shaded on one side, and lower branches may be physically damaged by contact with the wall.

As a rough rule of thumb, do not plant a tree nearer to a building than one and half times the likely height of the tree. However, if you already have an established tree that is nearer than this do not worry unduly.

Too much shade

Once a tree matures it may cast too much shade underneath it to support plant growth, particularly if it has a spreading habit and a dense leaf canopy. Grass in particular suffers when shaded by trees, so it is best to remove a large area and replace with bark chips rather than persevere with the grass. Trees with small leaves or a light canopy such as birch or *Robinia pseudoacacia* 'Frisia' cast only a light dappled shade that offers plenty of scope for under-planting.

Laburnums are justifiably widely planted, as they are among the most beautiful of all trees when in full flower. The one illustrated is *L.* x *watereri*, but grow the variety *L.* x w. 'Vossii' for a really super show.

The various varieties of *Acer palmatum* make excellent container trees, but young specimens should be given a sheltered position as young growth can be damaged by late frosts and cold spring winds.

patios and containers

Many Japanese maples make ideal container trees, although they can be expensive and need careful looking after, especially when young. The one illustrated is *Acer palmatum dissectum*.

The idea of growing trees in containers is not new, but it has become increasingly popular in recent years as gardens have become smaller and more use is made of patios. By growing a tree in a container of compost, rather than planting it out in the ground, you restrict the rootball and so the overall height and spread of the tree is reduced too. Container growing also makes it possible to grow trees near buildings in sites such as roof gardens, courtyards, doorways, or balconies.

Almost any tree could be grown in a container of a suitable size, but there are some species that have particular merit when grown this way.

In general, the slow-growers with a reasonable amount of drought tolerance fare best. From an aesthetic point of view, trees that do not look too lanky and bare at the base are the best.

Trees for containers

The following species are those in the Plant Directory that are most suitable for growing in containers. There are other possible trees, such as more tender types like *Citrus* that are beyond the scope of this book, but could be considered if you have a conservatory or greenhouse to overwinter them, or if you live in a frost-free climate.

Amelanchier lamarckii
Caragana arborescens 'Pendula'
Cotoneaster 'Hybridus Pendulus'
Crataegus oxyacantha
Ilex aquifolium
Juniperus scopulorum 'Skyrocket'
Laburnum x watereri 'Vossii' (for a limited time)
*Malus floribunda**
Malus 'John Downie'**
*M. tschonoskii**
Robinia pseudoacacia 'Frisia' (for a limited time)
Prunus 'Amanogawa'
Prunus cerasifera 'Nigra'
Prunus 'Kiku-shidare-zakura'
Prunus subhirtella
Pyrus salicifolia 'Pendula'
Salix caprea 'Kilmarnock' ('Pendula')
Sorbus vilmorinii
Taxus baccata 'Fastigiata'

* *Malus* used in containers should have been grafted onto a very dwarfing rootstock— check with your supplier.

When grouping plants together in pots, it is more successful to grow each as a single subject in its own pot, then group the pots, rather than grow a mixture of plants in one large container. However, in really small areas, a large tub with a tree under-planted with bulbs and ivy can work well.

Most kinds of birch (*Betula*) are likely to grow too large for a small garden, but a very large container will restrict their growth. Choose one trained into a multistemmed tree for most impact.

When it comes to arranging container plants the same principles apply as for border plantings. Choose a backbone of woody subjects including both deciduous and evergreens type, then look for contrasts of form and foliage to provide the impact rather than rely on flowering alone. Use smaller pots full of bedding or bulbs to add seasonal highlights and remove them from the scene once past their best.

A pair of containers either side of an entrance or at the top of steps works well with formal shapes like upright conifers or clipped evergreens like holly.

It is important that the roots are restricted but not potbound, so in the early years you should gradually move trees from the pots in which they were originally planted into containers up to 18 in. (45 cm) in diameter.

The final container will be at least 2 ft. (60 cm) in diameter and depth. Wooden half barrels are often used successfully, and there is a growing range of attractive plastic pots. Terra cotta is very expensive in these larger sizes, and there is always the risk it will not be frost-resistant despite claims to the contrary. Any container used will need drainage holes to prevent waterlogging of the compost, and it's worth raising the pot off the ground slightly.

It has to be said there are a few drawbacks to growing trees in containers. The main one is that trees are likely to be more short-lived than they would be in the ground. Aftercare, particularly watering, becomes more important. *See pages 44–45 for details.*

buy & plant

Trees are grown and offered for sale in two main forms: as bare-rooted plants or as container-grown plants in pots. **Bare-rooted trees** are grown by a nursery in open ground, then lifted during the dormant season. The soil falls away from the roots, leaving them exposed; there is some damage to the roots during lifting and handling. However, if the plant has a decent amount of root, this is protected from drying out with damp newspaper or similar material; the plant is handled with care and dispatched promptly to the customer. Such plants establish well and are much cheaper than container-grown plants. Being lighter, it is more feasible to buy these from specialized growers who will mail them to you.

Larger trees, especially conifers or evergreens over 5 ft. (1.5 m) can be offered as **"rootballed"** trees. These are grown in a similar way to bare-rooted trees but dug up with soil around the roots, which are wrapped in burlap or plastic.

Most trees on sale in garden centers will be ready-trained and container-grown. If you buy by mail, the trees are much more likely to be younger and bare-rooted.

(*For more details see pages 22–25.*)

shopping at garden centers

A typical garden center will have a fairly modest selection of tree species, although most of these should be suitable for small to medium gardens. The trees will have already been trained and pruned either to a full standard size (a clear stem of 6–6½ ft. [1.8–2.1 m]) or half standard (a clear stem of 4–5 ft. [1.2–1.5 m]). When it comes to buying conifers, you may have a choice of smaller younger plants or more mature specimens. It is worth remembering that younger plants are not only cheaper but soon catch up with more mature specimens as their root systems establish better. (Garden centers are not the places to go for much younger trees that you can train yourself—for this you need a tree specialist.)

The main display of trees will be arranged in alphabetical order by Latin name; usually the deciduous species are kept separate from the conifers. In addition to the main display, there is an increasing trend for garden centers to position plants in prominent beds at the entrance during their peak season of interest. So, for example, if you want to buy a magnolia look out for them in the months they flower.

Container-grown trees will be on sale all through the year but often the widest choice and freshest plants will be available in the spring. In general, avoid buying trees in the height of summer as the roots can become very stressed in the compost at this time.

As the majority of garden centers buy their trees from wholesale growers, it is important to choose an outlet with a high turnover of stock. Avoid trees that have been left sitting in their pots for more than two growing seasons. Those with faded labels, split pots, weedy compost, and poor plant growth should all be avoided. When plants are left out on display for more than a growing season they start to suffer from stress. Typically, they run short of water and nutrients in the small volume of compost, which can lead to severe wilting, premature flowering, or discolored foliage. (*For more advice on choosing good specimens see pages 26–27.*)

It's a good sign if the trees are clearly displayed, well labeled, and securely supported. But don't forget that most garden centers are happy to order a particular tree if it's not on display.

Garden centers throughout the world may vary in the kind of garden trees they sell, but you're almost sure to find plenty of choice. If in doubt about the suitability of a particular tree, ask an experienced member of staff

buy & plant

You are likely to need some help when buying a large item like a tree, so avoid visiting garden centers when they are busy. Peak times are spring holidays and weekends, particularly when the weather is good. Take advantage of late-night hours and rainy days to get the most help from staff.

If you want advice, make sure you get a knowledgeable member of staff to assist you. Don't be shy about checking the tree and picking a good specimen (*for specific tips see pages 26–27*). Ask for assistance to take the tree to the checkout—some may let you take the label to the checkout and then will deliver the tree for you.

Getting your tree home

You may be able to get a small tree in your car, but there is the risk of the branches getting damaged or the compost falling out of the pot. Don't be tempted to transport a tree on a roof rack or in an open trailer—it may suffer from severe desiccation which will check its growth when planted.

Most garden centers will deliver your tree for you within a couple of days for a small charge.

Guarantees

Most large garden centers offer a two-year guarantee on hardy plants such as trees, so it is worth keeping your receipt just in case you experience a problem. Such a guarantee does not affect your statutory rights but it is a sign that any complaint will be treated sympathetically—normally you will be offered a replacement or your money back.

buying from tree specialists

For a greater range of tree species and sizes you can use a tree specialist, either visiting in person or buying by mail order. There are various types of specialists ranging from keen amateurs with a small nursery in their garden to large wholesalers that supply garden centers. You can find out about them from advertisements in gardening publications, personal recommendations from gardening friends, stands at garden shows, and from publications such as *The Plant Finder* in the UK (there are similar publications in other countries).

There are nurseries that specialize in supplying unusual plants by mail order; these cover all plants, not just trees. They are useful if you are restocking a garden, as once you spend over a certain amount shipping is free. Many nurseries specialize in growing only trees and these offer the widest choice of species and specimens at various stages of growth. The trees are supplied bare-rooted or container-grown. Some outlets specialize even in certain groups such as conifers, maples, or *Prunus*.

Nurseries that supply young bare-rooted plants for hedges by mail order may offer a limited selection of plants, particularly native trees. Mail-order plants are only likely to be supplied during the dormant season and will be small and may need training; however, they are economical.

At the other extreme, some suppliers offer mature specimens in extra-large containers. Their main customers are landscapers and garden designers who want large one-of-a-kind specimens for garden shows and the like, but many will deal with the public. Typically, containers are around 18 in. (45 cm) in diameter and hold 12 gallons (45 l) of compost, which allows them to support trees over 7 ft. (2.1 m). Such trees might be around ten years old. As the stock is grown in containers, the outlets are open all year round and are not weather dependent. Most suppliers produce a catalog, but as the trees are so expensive, visit the outlet and check out the specimen in person (the supplier will usually deliver the tree at a later date).

When shopping for trees, don't expect to see all of the characteristics of the mature plants on a young specimen. The full beauty of the bark (this is snakebark maple) may only develop with age.

Always unpack mail order plants on arrival. If you can't plant them where you want them straight away, plant them temporarily in a spare piece of ground, or pot up small specimens.

Ordering by mail

An up-to-date copy of *The Plant Finder*, or its equivalent, is a quick starting point to track down desired plants (you will need to know the Latin name). It is now available on CD-ROM which makes it much quicker to locate a supplier, but of course you need a suitable computer. Contact the nursery for a catalog and to check the latest information on hours, availability, and delivery—many now have fax or e-mail.

Using catalogs to order a tree which is then delivered to your door can be an easy option if you follow a few basic guidelines. Most orders are processed and delivery takes place in the dormant season (autumn to winter), but it is usually best to order well in advance when the catalog comes out as orders are often processed in rotation.

Specify at the time of ordering whether you will accept substitutes or not. Also, when you are ordering remember to supply any relevant information such as dates on which you cannot accept delivery or where plants should be left if you are not there. It is always worth keeping copies of correspondence.

Unpack the item immediately after it is delivered. If you can't plant them at once, bare-rooted plants need potting up or heeling in to protect the exposed roots. If left unopened in warm, wet conditions the tree may start to grow but will be drawn and leggy through lack of light.

Contact the supplier as soon as possible if there is a problem such as inadequate or dried-out roots or plants that are so small they need to be potted up before planting outside. Keep records of telephone conversations and copies of correspondence. In many areas, you are entitled by law to a refund, and are not obliged to accept an offer of credit or replacement, if the plants are of poor quality or not as described.

choosing a
good specimen

It pays to take a bit of extra care choosing a good-quality tree. Here are the main points to check.

Container-grown

Look for a tree with a straight and even stem or trunk. The top growth should be balanced and well-shaped, not lopsided. Where trees have been displayed very close together, you will need to pull out several specimens so you can judge the shape easily.

It is important that the tree has established roots in the pot, which usually takes about twelve weeks during the growing season. After all, there's no point paying over the odds for a bare-rooted tree simply because it has been stuck in a pot of compost. A simple check is to lift the tree up by the trunk—if there is a reasonable rootball it should hold the tree in its pot.

At the other end of the spectrum, avoid a tree that has been stuck in the same pot for several seasons and has become potbound. Weedy or split pots, faded labels, and roots growing out of the drainage holes into the gravel beds are all warning signs. A potbound plant will have a very tangled root system with the main roots encircling the pot. These plants are a poor buy because when the tree is planted out into open ground, the roots will not spread out to anchor the plant through a well-developed root system. Also, the roots can become so entangled with each other they can't perform their function of taking up water and nutrients efficiently, leading to loss of vigor for the whole plant. Ideally, do not buy a tree that has been potbound, but if this is not possible then cut out the spiraling roots so that new ones will grow outward.

The top growth should look healthy and vigorous. Foliage should have no widespread unnatural tinges of yellow or red. In particular, inspect the young foliage for pests and diseases.

If growing apples in pots, be sure to buy one grown on a very dwarfing rootstock. Let your supplier know that you want to grow it in a container, and ask specifically for a dwarf rootstock.

Shape is especially important if you want to grow your tree in a container. This Japanese maple, *Acer palmatum dissectum*, is a good choice because it's usually bushy at the base.

buy & plant

Bare-rooted

There is not the same opportunity to inspect bare-rooted specimens as these are usually chosen by the supplier and dispatched by mail order. Some companies have a better reputation for quality control in this area than others, and it is not just a matter of the size and shape of the trees and its roots, but also how it is handled and cared for between being lifted from the ground and replanted. The time between lifting and replanting should be as short as possible, during which time the roots should be protected with damp newspaper or straw, or breathable plastic bag, and the tree kept cool but frost-free.

Conifers

Look for a symmetrical shape that is well-clothed with healthy foliage. Avoid trees with bare patches or browning of the foliage.

Phytophthora is a serious fungal disease that attacks conifers and is often fatal, so avoid trees infected with it. It is noticeable as a general browning of the foliage from the base upward. As it is spread by contaminated water, do not buy conifers that are left to sit in water or have a thick layer of liverwort on the surface of the compost.

When choosing between rootballed conifers, opt for the one with the largest rootball and where the covering is secure and intact.

Grafted trees

If a tree has been grafted onto a different rootstock, the union should have healed well with no more than a slight bend in it. Ornamental trees are usually grafted near to the ground but pendulous trees are grafted higher up the stem (this is sometimes called "topwork"). With grafted trees, look out for suckers growing from the rootstock, as they might overrun the scion unless removed.

Heavy clay soils

**Most trees will take longer to establish
on a heavy clay soil as it is so difficult for
the roots to penetrate, so try to improve
the drainage before planting. The tree
should be planted at the same level as it
was in the nursery but plant young trees
on a mound of improved soil to give them
a greater depth in which to root before
having to cope with wet clay.**

SUITABLE TREES

Abies	**Magnolia**
Amelanchier	**Malus**
Crataegus	**Prunus**
Ilex	**Salix**
Juniperus	**Sorbus**
Laburnum	**Ulmus**

Wet boggy soils

**Only a few trees from the Plant Directory
can cope with a wet soil, the main problem
being waterlogging of the roots and a lack
of oxygen. In very wet bog-like conditions
only a handful of tree species will be suitable.**

SUITABLE TREES

Amelanchier	**Pyrus**
Crataegus	**Salix**

Dry sandy soil

**Trees will be slower to establish and to put
on growth in these soils, lack of moisture
being the main limiting factor, but soluble
nutrients such as nitrogen quickly drain
away too. When planting on free-draining
sandy soils, incorporate slow-release general
fertilizers and plant the tree into a small
depression so water drains into the soil
around the root zone rather than runs off.**

SUITABLE TREES

Betula	**Ilex aquifolium**
Cercis	**Juniperus**
Cotoneaster	**Pyrus**
Crataegus	**Robinia**
Fagus	**Sorbus**

problem soils and sites

All the trees listed in the Plant Directory are hardy in most of North America and the UK, and so can be planted in the dormant season (autumn to spring) if bare-rooted, or at any time of year if container-grown. However, the soil and site can influence planting time too. For example, where the ground is very free-draining, such as in sandy or chalky soil, trees can run short of moisture during their first two seasons. Autumn planting can help ensure some root growth takes place before the onset of winter, which gives the tree a head start the following spring. It pays to wait until spring when planting evergreens in exposed locations, and that also applies to plants of borderline hardiness in cold areas and when having to plant in a wet, heavy clay soil.

Although container-grown plants can be planted all year-round, very dry soils and frozen soil make planting and aftercare hard work, so when the soil conditions are extreme, planting is best avoided.

Most soils can be improved by annual applications of well-rotted organic matter such as garden compost or farmyard manure. The organic matter provides humus which helps retain moisture in free-draining soils and prevent waterlogging in heavy clay soils. Coarse sand is often recommended to improve the drainage of heavy clay soils, but it is heavier to dig in than organic matter and can be expensive, so it is most feasible to do this over small areas.

It is worth remembering that growing trees in large tubs of compost is an alternative way of coping with problem soils, although problems associated with frost pockets are more likely.

Frost pockets

Even when a plant is hardy, late frosts can catch young spring growth or spring flowers, and this can disfigure the plant, although the effect is only temporary.

Thin chalky soils

Where there is a thin layer of topsoil over chalk, many trees struggle to make decent specimens. However, a deep soil over chalk is a different matter, with most trees able to thrive. Annual additions of organic matter or ordinary topsoil to the surface can help improve a tree's chances of developing well.

SUITABLE TREES

Acer griseum	**Fagus**
Arbutus unedo	**Juniperus**
(an ericaceous	**Laburnum**
plant that is lime	**Malus**
tolerant)	**Prunus**
Caragana arborescens	**Pyrus**
Crataegus	**Rhus**

Cold windy sites

Recently-planted trees may need to be sheltered for the first two years, either with a hedge or a temporary windbreak that filters the wind. Double-staking might be necessary (see pages 38–39). Evergreens can suffer in cold windy sites; large-leaved specimens are also at risk of being disfigured.

SUITABLE TREES

Betula pendula	**Juniperus**
Crataegus	**Laburnum**
Fagus	**Salix**
Ilex aquifolium	**Ulmus**

Coastal sites

Seaside winds carry salt spray which can damage foliage of sensitive plants. Double-staking might be necessary (see pages 38–39).

SUITABLE TREES

Acer griseum	**Ilex aquifolium**
Arbutus unedo	**Juniperus**
Cotoneaster	**Pyrus**
Crataegus	**Ulmus**

buy & plant

Planting a container-grown tree

1 Water the plant thoroughly and allow to drain while you are preparing the hole. Remove any turf or weeds, to create a clear area 3 ft. (90 cm) in diameter.

2 Dig out a large hole, twice the size of the tree's rootball. Put the topsoil to one side. If you are using soil improvers and fertilizers mix them in with the topsoil.

3 Trees over 4 ft. (1.2 m) can benefit from staking. It can be done at this stage to avoid root damage by inserting a stake just off-center on the side that gets the wind (see pages 38–39).

planting

The traditional wisdom has been to mix in plenty of organic soil improver with the soil when planting a tree and slow-release fertilizers such as bone meal were often suggested as well. Many gardeners feel comfortable with this advice, given the price of trees and that this is the one-and-only opportunity to improve the soil without damaging the tree roots. However, in recent years a number of studies on tree and shrub planting have shown that mulching and reducing competition from nearby vegetation such as grass and weeds contributes more to successful tree establishment than soil improvement.

Many gardeners now wish to reduce their use of peat as a planting medium for environmental reasons. There have also been, albeit unofficial, safety concerns over the use of bone meal. So the soil improvement and fertilizer additions are really a matter of personal conviction. The key point is to give the tree a chance to establish without competition for the first two years and to use mulches which will suppress weeds and help to retain moisture.

Container-grown trees

Container-grown plants make life easier as the planting season is much more flexible. They have their own root system encased in compost, so they can be planted at any time when the soil is workable, which means not cold and waterlogged, dust-dry, or frozen solid. Provided the tree was not potbound, it should be more successful at establishing itself than an equivalent bare-rooted tree.

The key point is to water plants thoroughly before planting so the compost is fully wetted, and to dig a large planting hole to take the rootball comfortably.

6 Once the tree is at the correct level, backfill with topsoil, firming it down gently with your foot as you go along. The aim is to remove any large air pockets and ensure the roots make contact with soil, but not to compress the soil too hard.

7 Trees that are to be staked need a tree tie to secure the tree to the stake. If necessary, protect the young bark from rabbits or other damage with a tree guard.

8 Water the tree in well. Lay down a circle of sheet mulch and disguise with a thin layer of chipped bark.

In areas prone to dry spells, a length of pipe can be laid around the rootball with one end open at the soil surface. During dry spells, water can be poured down the open end directly to the rootball.

4 Remove the tree from its container and gently tease out any roots growing around in a circle with a hand rake. If they have become too woody to do this, cut them off with pruning shears.

5 Add some of the topsoil to the bottom of the hole. Position the tree in the hole and use a bamboo cane or piece of wood to check the planting depth—the tree needs to be planted at the depth it was growing in the pot. Adjust the depth by adding or removing topsoil from under the rootball. This is tedious but worthwhile, so spend time getting it right, but don't let the rootball dry out in the meantime.

buy & plant

planting bare-rooted trees

The planting of bare-rooted trees is restricted to the dormant season and should be completed as soon as possible after lifting to prevent drying and damage to the roots.

Deciduous trees are best lifted and planted after they have shed their leaves (usually mid- or late autumn). Evergreens are better planted either earlier in the autumn or in mid-spring. At this time their roots are active so can replace the moisture lost by the foliage. Deciduous trees, like magnolias, with thick fleshy roots that are prone to rotting in cold wet soils, are often more successful when planted at the evergreen planting time.

Between lifting and planting, the tree needs to be protected from cold winds or strong sunshine. Keep the tree in a cool but frost-free place such as a porch, greenhouse, garage, or garden shed. The roots should be kept slightly moist—damp straw was used in the past but today a plastic bag is more convenient. If the tree cannot be planted for more than a few days, place the roots in a bucket of moist peat or compost.

When you have a lot of bare-rooted plants and are not able to plant them out straightaway, it is worth "heeling" them in. This simply means digging a trench in a sheltered part of the garden where the soil is well drained. Set the plants at an angle and cover the roots with moist soil.

Planting rootballed trees

Keep the plant wrapped up until the last possible moment to protect the roots. Dig a planting hole about twice the size of the rootball. Set the topsoil to one side; if you are using soil improvers they can be mixed in. Place the tree in the hole, remove wrapping and allow the soil to fall away into the hole. Pull the wrapping out from under the tree and dispose of it. Backfill the hole with compost, firm gently, and water well.

1 New plastic or wood containers may need drainage holes drilled in them. Old containers will need scrubbing out with hot soapy water to prevent carry-over of pests and diseases.

2 Cover the drainage holes with old pottery shards to prevent the compost washing through or add an inch (2.5 cm) or more layer of gravel. Stand the container on bricks or special "feet" to aid drainage and prevent staining of the patio. Position the container in its final site before planting.

3 Fill the pot with your chosen compost. Small standard trees may need a stake, which can be inserted before planting.

4 Take the tree out of its pot and plant so that the soil mark on the stem is about 2 in. (5 cm) below the rim of the container. Firm the compost down gently as you go along using your hands.

5 Mulch to reduce the need to water: chipped bark, gravel, slate, or even pebbles all work well.

buy & plant

It's worth investing in an attractive container so that your potted tree makes a pleasing feature from the moment it's planted.

Trees in containers

A soil-based compost will add weight to the container, which is often useful with a top-heavy tree. It will also maintain its physical structure better if left outside year after year, unlike peat-based composts which can lose their structure in heavy winter rains unless mulched or protected. However, peat-based multipurpose compost can be used if you want easy-to-maneuver pots or if you are prepared to repot regularly. Make sure the plant is watered thoroughly before and after planting.

tree care

Despite the impact trees have on the garden, most require **minimal care** compared with cultivating smaller plants such as bedding or perennials. You are spared the annual ritual of preparing seedbeds, waiting for the last spring frosts, and nurturing small plants against relentless pest attacks. For the most part, tree care operates on a more relaxed timetable where checks are made either in the spring or during the dormant season.

The **essentials** you need to know to get your tree off to a **successful start** are covered in the following section of the book. Many of the techniques such as formative pruning you might not be familiar with, but they are straightforward if you understand why they are done. An interesting aspect of tree care is that new ways of doing things are constantly coming to light as research into forestry and commercial tree planting finds practical application in the home garden.

Vulnerable plants may benefit from wind protection such as burlap or horticultural fleece while young. When animals such as deer or rabbits are likely to be the problem, wire-netting may be more appropriate.

the early years

Once a tree has been planted the key tasks in the early years are watering, feeding, and weed control. Many of these tasks can be combined by appropriate mulching techniques. To care for your tree and protect it from unexpected events, it is worth looking at it regularly. For example, newly-planted trees often get lifted out of the ground after a spell of hard frost, and it is important to firm them gently back in position using your feet before the roots dry out. Evergreens or deciduous trees with young spring growth in exposed positions are best protected with a windbreak screen against cold winds, and you need to keep an eye on this to make sure it's still secure.

Watering

Where the soil remains moist you may get away without adding extra water, particularly if the tree has a good root system and was planted and mulched correctly. But you should check regularly for the first couple of years.

During dry spells, or where the ground is very free-draining, such as a sandy or chalky soil, some extra watering will be needed. The most efficient way to water is to apply a reasonable amount once a week rather than a light sprinkle every day. A reasonable amount would be about 3–8 gallons to 1 sq. yd. (14–40 liters/sq m) of ground surrounding the tree. A hose can be used instead but if the water comes out too forcefully it could wash away the soil. Water should be applied steadily, allowing time for it to soak into the ground before more is added.

To target water directly to the tree roots, a pipe can be inserted nearby at the time of planting. Water can then be poured down this pipe using a funnel, and thus gets exactly to where it is needed. The idea is worth trying for expensive trees or those where it's difficult to get a hose. A number of different pipes have been tried, from so called leaky hoses to tubes used for washing machines. Remember to cover the open end when not in use to prevent it gathering debris. Automatic irrigation systems are a possibility too, but as a long-term measure they are more appropriate to trees in containers.

Feeding

A tree growing in a reasonable garden soil (such as one that was previously cultivated with plenty of organic matter) does not need any additional fertilizer. Extra fertilizer could be beneficial on very free-draining ground such as dry sandy soils or unimproved chalky soils, as water passes through quickly taking soluble nutrients such as nitrogen with it. In such instances apply a general fertilizer with roughly equal amounts of nitrogen, phosphorus, and potassium, ideally one that releases the nitrogen slowly.

Fertilizer is usually applied as a powder or granules around the base of the tree in spring before mulching. It's important to apply when the soil is moist or when you can water well afterward as dry fertilizer can scorch roots.

Mulching with well-rotted organic matter will supply some nutrients, particularly if you use coconut shells, rotted farmyard manure, or garden compost.

tree care

Mulching

A mulch will suppress weeds and will also help keep the ground moist by reducing the amount of water evaporated from the soil surface. A mulch can be a loose material like chipped bark, gravel, coconut shells, manure, or leaf mold, laid at least 2 in. (5 cm) thick, or a sheet such as black polyethylene, woven polypropylene, or even newspaper.

Choose a material that fits the setting and make sure the area is weed-free before applying the mulch. A mulch will be most effective if it is put in place in early or mid-spring.

If a fairly large tree is planted, it may be advisable to use this kind of staking to hold the tree securely until it has rooted well into the surrounding soil. The stakes can then be removed.

stakes and supports

There are a lot of misconceptions about staking trees, perhaps because of the examples seen in parks and other public areas. The purpose of staking a tree is to hold the roots firm in the soil until new ones can grow and anchor themselves—it is not about holding the stem rigidly in place. Staking is essentially a short-term helping hand for two or three growing seasons, not a permanent fixture. There is no need to treat the stake with preservative; in fact it will be easier to remove if it has started to rot at the base.

Tall stakes are often used, but research has shown that short stakes, with no more than 1–1½ ft. (30–45 cm) above ground, are better for the development of the tree stem in the long term. A tree stem needs to be moved gently backward and forward by the wind to strengthen it. When the stem is held firmly in place by a tall stake, it doesn't get the chance to thicken and develop, and so is more likely to snap or fall over in a strong wind than an unstaked tree that is used to bending.

To minimize root damage, particularly for container-grown trees, it is best to insert the stake before planting. A stake 3 ft. (90 cm) long can be used with 2 ft. (60 cm) driven into the ground and the rest above. If a young tree was not staked at planting time but then needs a stake, drive one in to the ground at an angle of 45 degrees, so it leans into the wind.

The tree should be attached to the stake by a plastic tree tie (from garden centers). It is best to use a proprietary one (sometimes called buckler and spacer ties) as they are designed to stop the tree rubbing against the

If using a traditional stake close to the stem, keep it short, and be sure to use a tree tie that has a spacer to prevent damage from friction against the stake.

Staking drawbacks

One argument for not staking trees at all is that it is unnecessary—after all nature grows trees successfully without providing stakes! Young trees, such as you might buy from a tree nursery, and those under say 4 ft. (1.2 m), should not need staking at all. A stake can damage the tree by rubbing against it, or the tie can strangle a tree if not loosened, so once staked more checking is needed. Incorrect staking can make the tree more, not less, vulnerable to wind. So it is clear that staking should only be used where necessary—with trees over 4 ft. (1.2 m) when planted, or on exposed sites, and then only as a short-term measure.

stake and can be adjusted easily. The tie will need to be loosened as the girth of the tree increases, so remember to check it at the end of the growing season.

Large trees can be staked with two or three stakes, either opposite each other or spread around the trunk. Given that the rootball will be bigger, the stakes will be further from the stem, so use heavy-duty ties and nail them to the stake.

Thin-stemmed trees

When trees have been raised with unusually thin stems, as may be the case with some *Malus*, the stems do need some support in the early years. Either support them with a bamboo cane so the stem can move in the wind and thicken up, or use a tall stake for a single growing season, then cut this down and use it as a short stake for the second season. Finally remove it for the third growing season.

pruning and training

Established trees need little or no routine pruning except where there are dead, damaged, or diseased branches to tackle. However, particularly in a small garden, you might want a tree that has been shaped in its early years—this is known as formative pruning. For example, if it's left to its own devices, *Amelanchier lamarckii* forms a multistemmed large shrub, but formative pruning to encourage a single stem can produce a small tree.

How much formative pruning you need to do depends on the age of tree, how much was already done before you bought it, and what shape of tree you want. For container-grown trees around 6 ft. (1.8 m) high, as you might find in a garden center, some training will have already been done to form the stem and head. It is then a matter of choosing what shape is appropriate for the species (*see the individual entries in the Plant Directory for more details*) and following the instructions shown on the right.

Young trees

When you buy young trees (often called whips or maidens) from a hedging supplier or tree specialist you might have to do more of the formative pruning yourself. Start at ground level and remove two thirds of the sideshoots, but leave any leaf rosettes near the stem. In the second year repeat this process. From then on prune for shape (*see above*).

Feathered trees

These have a leading shoot clothed with sideshoots. During the dormant season cut back the sideshoots to within 2–4 in. (5–10 cm) of the main stem. If the side branches are overcrowded, remove the weakest ones.

Standards

Remove the sideshoots so there is a clear stem up to the head of the tree. Any leaf clusters that grow from the stem without forming a shoot should be left. Remove any other dominant shoot that threatens to compete with the leader.

Multistemmed

Trees with attractive bark are often grown this way. Specimens may be available already trained, or you can prune back hard a very young (maiden) tree to encourage two or three shoots to grow out from the base.

Weeping trees

Formative pruning has to create a clear stem tall enough to allow the branches to hang attractively, but as this is part of the selling feature most trees will be purchased with this pruning already done. If the weeping branches can benefit from trimming to improve the symmetry, cut out any inward-facing or upward-facing ones to create the best shape. To control the height, cut out the central leader above a branch and prune out any leader that forms afterward.

Removing a branch

To help form a longer clear stem on a young tree, cut some of the lower shoots back to the main stem.

Small branches can simply be sawed through, but larger ones should be removed in stages.

Pruning established trees

Little routine pruning is needed once a framework has been formed, but it is worth pruning out any dead, damaged, or diseased branches as they can spread problems to the rest of the tree as well as spoil the appearance.

Removing suckers

Where a tree has been grafted on to a different rootstock, there is always the risk that the rootstock will produce its own shoots. These suckers should be removed promptly as they will sap the strength from the main tree and could even outgrow it. Shoots may appear just beneath the graft union or they may come up from the roots some distance from the tree. Cut or pull the suckers off as close to their origin as possible and rub out any regrowth as soon as it appears.

When to prune

Prune at a convenient time in late autumn to winter. Some trees like *Acer*, *Betula*, and *Prunus* release a lot of sap when cut, so for these the best time is mid-summer. Evergreens are best pruned in late summer.

APHIDS

Look for colonies of greenfly, blackfly, or even pinkish bugs around leaves and young shoots. Serious infestations will weaken growth and could transmit viruses. Pinch out affected leaves if they can be reached safely; small trees could be sprayed with a suitable aphid killer.

CATERPILLARS

Ragged holes in young leaves are a sign that winter moths have laid eggs on the tree and the resulting grubs are feeding. Pick off any you can reach—spraying in spring often works well as their soft bodies are vulnerable to chemicals. To avoid problems, grease bands can be placed around the trunk in mid-autumn to prevent the female moths climbing up.

GALL MITES

Small reddish growths on the leaves look alarming but are usually harmless. Pick off affected leaves, or wait until the leaves fall and then burn them.

RED SPIDER MITES

Speckling or bronzing of young leaves from spring onward is the sign of these pests. Spray young trees after flowering with a suitable insecticide.

SCALE INSECTS

Colonies of brown, yellow, or white scales appear on older wood. They can be brushed off with warm, soapy water. You can apply a winter wash, or use a suitable insecticide in spring.

pest and disease control

Above: By the time the fruiting bodies of honey fungus (*Armillaria mellea*) can be seen the disease is already well established. To confirm diagnosis make the checks suggested opposite.

Opposite: Aphids such as blackfly can affect a wide range of trees. Here blackfly have started to colonize a laburnum.

Trees are better able than most garden plants to overcome problems with pests and diseases, partly on account of their size and longevity, but mainly because of the bark that forms a protective barrier. Trees are most at risk if this barrier is damaged, as there is then an entry point for diseases. Roots are another potential entry point for diseases.

If trouble does strike, whether you need to take action or not depends on the problem: long-term diseases like honey fungus and fire blight need prompt action. Some of the most common and serious problems are covered in the columns at right.

Larger pests

Pest problems are not confined to insects. Larger animals such as deer, squirrels, rabbits, and birds can cause damage if they visit your garden. Tree guards and netting may help protect young trees most at risk.

Diseases

BACTERIAL CANKER

Shallow patches appear on the bark of *Prunus* species in autumn/winter. By the spring there might be a brown gum oozing out. Prune out affected branches and spray with a copper-based fungicide.

BRACKET FUNGI

Toadstools that look like small shelves grow from the trunk or branches. Cut off affected branches. Where the fungus affects the trunk try to cut the fungus out, removing any rotting wood if this is practicable.

CORAL SPOT

Branches die back and red pustules are seen. Cut out dead wood, and as the fungus can spread to live wood too, cut back to about 6 in. (15 cm) below the disease. Burn the prunings.

FIRE BLIGHT

Branches die back, leaves turn brown and wither. Cankers may also be present. Prune out diseased wood 2 ft. (60 cm) back into healthy tissue. Burn the prunings.

FUNGAL CANKER

Oval cankers appear on the trunk and branches, often shrunken with the bark drying in rings. Cut out and burn affected material. Spray with copper-based fungicide in late summer.

HONEY FUNGUS

Leaves turn yellow and die off prematurely. Honey-colored toadstools may appear at the base of the trunk. Use a sharp knife to peel back some bark at the base of the tree; look for white fluffy growth. You may also see black "bootlaces" by which the fungus spreads, in the soil or under the bark. This is a serious disease for which there is no cure so the tree and its roots will have to be removed and burnt. Do not replant trees or shrubs on the site for at least a year, and thereafter only replant with those species that can tolerate it.

PHYTOPHTHORA

A fungus that attacks the roots causing the tree to be stunted with yellow foliage and die-back. It is most likely on very wet soils. Remove and burn the tree and its roots.

POWDERY MILDEW

White powdery coating on leaves and stems. Remove badly infected shoots and spray with a suitable fungicide, repeating if necessary.

RUST

Brown, orange, or yellow spots appear on leaves in summer. Pick off and burn affected leaves. The tree can be sprayed with a suitable fungicide.

SCAB

The leaves exhibit green blotches and fall early. Blister-like pimples develop on young shoots; cracks and scabs appear on the bark. Cut out affected growth and burn. Spraying at bud stage is worthwhile if you do it regularly. To prevent problems clear up fallen leaves in winter.

SILVER LEAF

This particularly affects *Prunus* species. The leaves have a silvery appearance, and a purple fungus may grow on dead wood. A section of wood may show brown or purple staining when moistened. Cut out the branches to 2 ft. (60 cm) below the stain, then use a wound sealant.

caring for trees in containers

While any tree you grow in a container will need more attention to keep it in tip-top condition than the same species grown in the open ground, most of the basic care such as pruning and spraying is often more manageable.

Watering and feeding

Growing a tree permanently in a container will restrict the spread of its roots so you will need to water and feed during the growing season throughout its life, not just in the early years.

A tree on a hot sunny patio may need watering twice a day in summer, so it is worth looking at ways to make this easier. Mulching each spring is particularly worthwhile, and using material such as gravel will also keep the rootball cool. Where there are numerous pots to water, or if you are often away from home, a simple automatic watering system could be the answer.

These consist of a water timer fitted near an outside tap that turns the water on and off at set times, and a series of pipes that carry the water to the pots, each pot being fitted with a small tube with an irrigation device at the end. They work well, but you need to allow time to set them up and try them out before going away.

The compost will only supply enough nutrients for four to six weeks, so after that you will need to add extra fertilizer. As a matter of routine, each spring remove any old mulch and the top 2 in. (5 cm) layer of compost with a hand rake or trowel. Replace with fresh multipurpose or potting

compost mixed with a general balanced fertilizer, or better still a modern slow-release fertilizer. Water in well and add the annual mulch.

Liquid feeds can be used instead of the top-dressing described above or as a supplement to it later in the season. There are various formulations—to encourage flowers and fruits a tomato feed can be used. Follow the instructions for the correct dose—if the concentration is too strong the roots could be scorched. It is better to apply a dilute liquid feed little and often rather than large doses infrequently.

Winter care

All the trees in this book are hardy, but even with these species there is a risk of the rootball freezing in the container during the winter. The larger the container the less susceptible it is to temperature changes, and some materials, such as wooden barrels, offer more protection than say plastic or terra cotta.

You may be able to move the pot to somewhere more sheltered for the winter, but an alternative is to wrap the outside of the pot in several layers of bubble insulation.

Heavy winter rains can cause the compost to become waterlogged, so try to provide protection as it is the effect of frozen waterlogged compost that can be fatal to the roots.

Repotting

After about four or five years you might notice a decline in health and vigor of the tree. This is a sign that it needs repotting into a larger container. A good time of year to do this is early to mid-spring, so that the tree is ready for the new growing season. With larger specimens or heavy containers it's worth getting help. Lay the container on its side: while one person holds it steady, the other can ease the tree out.

Use a hand rake to tease out the roots so they are not so congested, and dislodge some of the old compost. Cut off any over-long or spiraling roots with pruning shears. If it's not possible to pot the tree into a large container, then trim the whole rootball to reduce its size slightly and dislodge as much of the old compost as possible—the tree can then go back into its original container. Replant, putting in pottery shards or gravel as before and using fresh compost.

tree care

plant

directory

Most of the trees
mentioned in this
book are tough and
able to withstand low
temperatures, but if
you live in a cold part
of the world it's best
to make sure the
trees you choose are
likely to survive. Each
tree entry has been
given a hardiness
zone, so if in doubt
check with the table
below. These are the
average annual mini-
mum temperatures.

1 **Below -50°F**
   (-45.5°C)
2 **-50 to -40°F**
   (45.5 to -40.1°C)
3 **-40 to -30°F**
   (-40 to -34.5°C)
4 **-30 to -20°F**
   (-33.4 to -28.9°C)
5 **-20 to -10°F**
   (-28.8 to -23.4°C)
6 **-10 to 0°F**
   (-23.3 to -17.8°C)
7 **0 to +10°F**
   (-17.7 to -12.3°C)

plant directory

This young *Abies koreana* doesn't look very spectacular at this stage, but within a few years it will be bearing cones and is likely to become a focal point among your trees.

Abies koreana

If you have doubts about the value of conifers, grow this one. Although quite large ultimately, it's slow-growing and bears its wonderfully striking, large cones while still a very small tree. This evergreen is full of elegance, with a hint of grandeur that many other small trees lack.

Where conditions suit, this impressive conifer may ultimately exceed the height of most of the other trees in this book, but it's slow-growing and in most gardens is unlikely to grow taller than about 30 ft. (9 m), even after many years. After 10 years it may have attained only 6 ft. (1.8 m).

This fir tree almost always attracts favorable comment because of its shape and stature, even when young, but especially so when the cylindrical cones appear.

Attractive color

Close examination of the leaves (needles) will show that they are a dark, glossy green above but gleaming silvery-white below. It's a combination that's difficult to describe, but the two-tone effect is very striking and coupled with the tree's neat habit creates a very pleasing overall appearance. It's attractive all year round, but likely to be valued especially in winter when the majority of trees are denuded and stark.

Pleasing shape

Young trees soon begin to take on a conical shape, and by the time they are perhaps ten years old, the cone-shaped profile is especially pleasing, with the trunk clothed almost to ground level.

Interesting cones

It's undoubtedly the cones that make this one of the most desirable of the medium-sized conifers. They're large and conspicuous, and appear on young trees much sooner than on most conifers. This also means they're more likely to be at eye level rather than above head height.

The cylindrical cones, about 4 in. (10 cm) long and 1 in. (2.5 cm) across, are green to violet-purple at first, turning brown later.

Abies koreana is grown mainly for its very attractive cones. These are produced even while the tree is young, sometimes on specimens less than 3 ft. (1 m) tall.

POSSIBLE PROBLEMS

None likely, other than a poor shape if cramped by neighboring trees or shrubs.

BUYING TIP

You should be able to buy this as a container-grown plant in most good garden centers. Choose one that has a pleasing symmetrical shape with branches evenly distributed.

KEY FACTS

Soil
Ideally deep and moisture-retentive. Unlikely to do well on dry, shallow soils.

Site
Best in a sunny, open position.

Hardiness
Zone 5

Likely height
25–30 ft. (8–9 m)

plant directory

Abies koreana

This pleasing conifer is native to the peninsula of Korea and a few offshore islands, hence its common name of Korean fir.

Acer davidii

Snakebark maples are fascinating trees with interesting bark that often becomes a talking-point. They are grown primarily for the year-round interest provided by their bark, and for autumn foliage color. Several other acers , apart from *A. davidii*, have similar interesting bark.

Acer davidii, one of the best snakebark maples, is native to central China, and named after the French missionary the Abbé David who found it. In ideal conditions, and given sufficient time, it can become a medium-sized tree, but in most gardens it will remain small enough to qualify for inclusion here.

The greenish bark has fascinating vertical striations, which with a little imagination can be likened to a snake's skin. The green leaves are unlobed, unlike those of most acers, and are borne on reddish stalks; in autumn the foliage usually turns yellow before falling.

Left: It's easy to see why *Acer davidii* is described as one of the snakebark maples. The striated bark is a feature you can enjoy throughout all the seasons.

Right: The fruiting "keys" are an attractive bonus. Starting green, they slowly mature to a pink-suffused red.

Beautiful bark

Acer davidii is grown primarily for its attractive bark, so place it where this feature can be appreciated in winter. The striations usually begin to appear on wood that's at least two years old, and look best once the tree has a trunk with a reasonable girth.

Flowers and fruit

The yellowish mid-spring flowers are inconspicuous, but the green-winged seeds ("keys"), often tinged red, similar to those of the sycamore, are a bonus later in the year.

Autumn tints

Colorful foliage tints just before leaf-fall are a feature of most acers, but *A. davidii* is not especially vivid in coloring, although the leaves may turn yellow before they fall.

POSSIBLE PROBLEMS

You may have to be patient, especially if you buy a small specimen, as the snakebark effect may not be pronounced until the tree has been growing for about five years. This maple is not a good choice if you're looking for instant impact.

BUYING TIP

Although this is not rare tree, you may have to go to a specialist tree nursery to buy them. If you want to appreciate their beautiful bark sooner rather than later, consider buying a fairly large specimen—though this will naturally cost you more.

BEAUTIFUL BARK

The snakeskin-like bark is appreciated best in winter, when most other trees can be a little boring. It make take a few years before the effect is really striking, so be patient while the tree is still young.

Soil
**Best on moist but
well-drained
ground.**

Site
**Best in full sun,
but will grow well
in light shade.**

Hardiness
Zone 6

Likely height
25 ft. (8 m)

plant directory

Acer davidii

Several types of acer
are called snakebark
maples, for reasons
already described.
This particular snake-
bark is known by the
common name Père
David's maple.

51

Acer griseum

This is a wonderful tree that always looks interesting, whatever time of year you admire it... and it's slow-growing so won't readily outstay its welcome. Unfortunately this same characteristic means that you have to be patient to appreciate it's full impact!

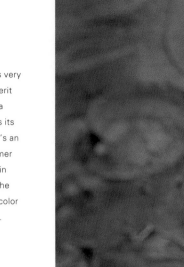

Acer griseum is very much a multimerit tree. Although a stunning bark is its main feature, it's an attractive summer tree and super in autumn when the leaves change color before they fall.

The peeling cinnamon-colored bark is perhaps the main reason for choosing this tree, but it's a good all-rounder that has other pleasing attractions.

A native of central China, it seems to thrive in cultivation. It's sometimes seen as a multistemmed tree or large shrub, but grow it with a clear single trunk for maximum impact as a specimen tree to admire.

Peeling bark

Sometimes called a paperbark maple, because the outer layer of bark peels off like sheets of brown paper, a mature tree makes an especially eye-catching feature when its trunk it highlighted in winter sunshine.

You may have to wait a few years for maximum effect. The brown bark does not normally start to peel before the wood is three or four years old, then it flakes off to reveal the golden-brown beneath.

Flowers and seeds

The pendulous sulphur-yellow flowers in early spring are small but nevertheless a welcome bonus, while the twin-winged "keys" that help to distribute the seeds in the wind are pleasingly attractive at close-quarters. Don't expect to benefit from these added attractions while the tree is still young.

Autumn color

The summer foliage is olive to gray-green, but toward the end of the season it turns glowing shades of autumnal red and orange. The tree is often seen as its best as low late sunshine brings out the autumn foliage coloring and spotlights the flaking bark below.

POSSIBLE PROBLEMS

Slow growth means that you'll have to be patient to see the benefits of planting this beautiful tree, but it's worth the wait. It may be necessary to remove low-growing shoots and branches to ensure a clear trunk is established.

BUYING TIP

You may have to go to a good garden center or specialist tree nursery... and expect this specimen to cost more than many of the commoner trees. Propagation is from seed, and slow germination and subsequent slow growth mean this is more expensive to propagate and grow to a size suitable for sale than many other trees.

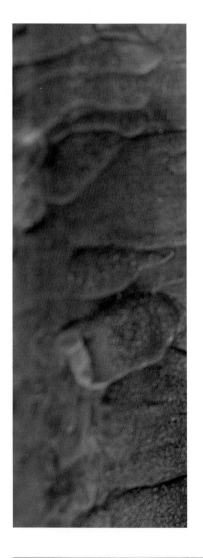

Soil
Undemanding, and will even do well in chalky gardens. Moist but well-drained ground is likely to produce faster growth.

Site
Best in full sun, but will tolerate light shade.

Hardiness
Zone 5

Likely height
20 ft. (6 m)

plant directory

Acer griseum

It's easy to see why *A. griseum* gets the name paperbark maple. The old bark peels back like brown paper to expose the cinnamon-colored new bark beneath.

Acer palmatum 'Atropurpureum'

Surely one of the most beautiful trees for a small garden, this tree never fails to impress with its shapely outline and wonderful color. And it is just one of many varieties with interesting leaf shapes and colors.

You may find this wonderful plant in shrub books as well as those describing trees—it all depends on how it's been trained and whether or not it's a mature specimen. With age it will make an exceptionally beautiful tree, usually with only a very short trunk, or with multiple stems arising from close to ground level. In leaf it can make a tight mound of foliage that almost obscures the branches and from a distance it can often look like a large shrub.

Unfortunately, it's not the easiest tree to grow if you live in a cold or exposed area, and may require coaxing during the early years. But the reward are worth it.

Grow more than one variety if you have the space and are able to offer suitable conditions, for these beautiful acers will certainly make an eye-catching contribution to your garden.

Purple leaves

The ordinary species has green leaves that age to bronze or purple toward autumn, but 'Atropurpureum' has deep purple foliage throughout spring and summer. 'Bloodgood' is another especially choice variety, with red new growth that ages to an almost blackish-purple by autumn, followed by the usual firework display of colors before the leaves fall.

There are other varieties in shades of yellow as well as bronze-green and purple, some with leaves more finely dissected.

The small but insignificant flowers in spring are followed by the usual acer "keys," but these trees are grown purely for foliage effect.

Red and scarlet autumn tints

The already colorful foliage becomes even more spectacular before it falls, often creating a flaming display that shouts for attention even from across the garden. The effect can be especially stunning if the tree is planted near a pond where the reflection can double the impact.

Acer palmatum 'Dissectum Atropurpureum' makes a graceful tree, with more finely divided leaves than 'Atropurpureum.'

Even in summer before the autumn colors develop, all acers makes beautiful specimen trees, planted in a border or standing alone.

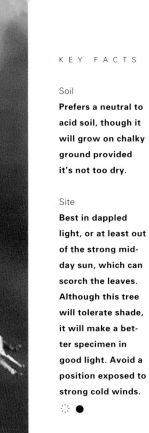

Soil
Prefers a neutral to acid soil, though it will grow on chalky ground provided it's not too dry.

Site
Best in dappled light, or at least out of the strong midday sun, which can scorch the leaves. Although this tree will tolerate shade, it will make a better specimen in good light. Avoid a position exposed to strong cold winds.

Hardiness
Zone 5

Likely height
15 ft. (4.5 m)
Varieties with dissected foliage may be only half this height.

Acer palmatum 'Atropurpureum' has purple summer foliage, but in autumn the leaves turn all the colors associated with this time of year.

POSSIBLE PROBLEMS

Spring growth, especially on young trees, may be damaged by cold winds and late spring frosts. The new leaves may be killed, but new growth often makes good the early damage. The cut-leaved varieties such as 'Dissectum Atropurpureum' are particularly vulnerable. Very strong sunshine can also damage immature leaves by scorching them.
It may be necessary to remove some of the lower shoots as the plant grows, to encourage a more tree-like shape.

BUYING TIP

These trees can resent disturbance, so buy container-grown plants. To grow as a tree, choose one with a reasonably straight stem with a tendency to grow upright rather than branch out.

plant directory

Acer palmatum **'Atropurpureum'**

The popular name of Japanese maple is potentially misleading, as other acers share the same common name, especially *A. japonicum* in its many forms.

Amelanchier lamarckii

This tree comes in many guises, sometimes as a large shrub, sometimes as a single-trunked or multistemmed tree. There is even confusion about the name, with one species often masquerading as another. However, it matters not a bit if you're looking for a good garden plant, for all of them are delightful multimerit trees that are unlikely to outgrow their welcome in a small garden.

These North American and Canadian natives are now naturalized in many parts of Europe, and over the years some have been distributed to gardeners under incorrect names due to the confused nomenclature (see box). *A. lamarckii* is probably the best to choose as a small garden tree, with *A. laevis* a close second. The true *A. canadensis* is a more of a suckering shrub, but in some European countries *A. laevis* may have been distributed under this name.

Don't let this complicated history deter you from buying any of the amelanchiers. They are sure to grace your garden and their varied performance from spring to autumn won't disappoint.

The pale gray winter shoots are transformed in mid-spring by the emerging delicate pink to copper-bronze young foliage, followed almost immediately by a frothy mass of pure white flowers. These can be fleeting, lasting perhaps a week in warm or windy weather, but then you can enjoy the fresh young leaves as they continue to enlarge and gradually turn green.

Juneberries

By late spring and early summer the flowers are just a memory, but in favorable conditions you'll become aware of the ripening berries, turning from red to purple-black as they mature.

Autumn fling

There's a final bid for attention before the leaves drop in autumn, when they often color wonderfully. *A. laevis* is especially good for autumn color, with shades of soft red to orange, often with hints of yellow and brown—a showy performance that's often relatively long-lasting.

Right: The spring display of white flowers is relatively brief, and the tree may look at its most spectacular for about a week, but its impact more than makes up for this.

Left: Although individual leaves are small, amelanchers make a showy display of autumn color—they both start and end the season with a spectacular show.

Above: The actual intensity of the autumn color depends to some extent on the season, but amelanchiers can be relied upon to give a pleasing final fling before the leaves drop.

Soil
Undemanding, but thrives best in a well-drained soil that's not too dry.

Site
Best in full sun but still grows well in partial shade. Does less well in shade.

Hardiness
Zone 4

Likely height
25 ft. (8 m)

POSSIBLE PROBLEMS

Tree forms are sometimes grafted onto a rootstock of hawthorn (*Crataegus laevigata*) or pear (*Pyrus communis*). These sometimes root poorly and produce suckers (shoots from the roots), which should be removed at source if they appear.
No routine pruning is required, but it may be necessary to remove low branches as the tree grows. Multistemmed trees (which have several main branches from the base) can be attractive, and you may prefer not to reduce these to a simple main stem.

BUYING TIP

You should be able to find amelanchiers in large garden centers, but they will often be shrubby plants with lots of branches from near the base. Tree forms will have been trained in the nursery by having sideshoots low down on the main stem removed to produce a clear "leg." If you have difficulty finding one trained like this, order from a mail-order nursery.

plant directory

Amelanchier lamarckii

In Great Britain, common names include Juneberry (alluding to the fruits), snowy mespilus (mespilus being one of its old botanical names), and service berry. In America it's known as shadbush or shadblow, as well as service berry.

Arbutus unedo

This is one of the few flowering evergreen trees suitable for a small garden, and if you're patient enough it will make a superb specimen tree that's sure to attract plenty of attention. Unfortunately, it's not a good choice for cold, exposed gardens.

This slow-growing tree is sometime seen looking more like a large shrub, but in time it will make a choice wide-topped small tree. A native of the Mediterranean region and southwest Ireland, it's relatively cold-tolerant, though a favorable position will ensure a better-shaped tree and more rapid growth.

A multimerit tree, it has late flowers and fruits resembling strawberries—both at the same time!

Evergreen leaves

Dark, shiny, and leathery-looking evergreen leaves, resembling those of a bay tree, make this a good choice where a year-round focal point is required, and is useful where you need something that looks clothed in winter. It's not a particularly useful choice if you want a tree to screen an unattractive outlook, however, as it's too slow-growing to provide quick cover.

Pitcher-shaped flowers

The drooping clusters of white or pinkish pitcher-shaped flowers are produced in late autumn and are often still present in early winter. Although not large, and inconspicuous from a distance, they add interest at a time of year when flowers are especially scarce.

Arbutus unedo rubra has pinkish-red flowers, but it may not be quite as hardy and vigorous as the white-flowered species.

Strawberry-like fruit

The orange-red strawberry-like fruits (perhaps more like cherries with rough, pimply skins) are not often produced in abundance, but they're especially eye-catching. They ripen a year after the flowers are produced, which is why they appear together.

Being edible, although bland, the fruits are used to make a liqueur in some countries.

POSSIBLE PROBLEMS

The most likely complaint is slow growth. These trees take time to establish, and even an older one grows only slowly. It may exceed the 15 ft. (4.5 m) mentioned above, but only after a long time, and in favorable conditions. Very biting cold winter winds may damage the foliage, but the tree is likely to grow out of this by the following summer.

BUYING TIP

Always buy container-grown specimens, and expect to have to shop around to find a garden center that stocks it. You may have to buy from a specialist tree nursery.

Soil
Tolerates most soils, including chalky ground. A soil with a high organic content is likely to produce better growth, however.

Site
Light shade is ideal, but full sun is tolerated. Although tolerant of coastal regions, avoid cold areas inland.

Hardiness
Zone 7

Likely height
15 ft. (4.5 m)

The flowers of *Arbutus unedo* are interesting rather than beautiful. They are produced, sometimes in profusion, in late autumn and early winter.

A mature specimen may carry a conspicuous display of fruits, which make a more prominent display than the flowers from a distance.

Although the fruits are edible, they are bland, barely succulent, and generally not to be recommended. Just enjoy them as a decorative feature.

plant directory

Arbutus unedo

A. *unedo.* is commonly called the strawberry tree, the name alluding to the red fruits.

Betula pendula 'Youngii'

The graceful and fast-growing birches are popular trees, but most of them quickly grow too tall for a small garden. This weeping form is an elegant tree that's unlikely to become a problem.

The size, stature, and gracefulness of this charming tree makes it instantly appealing, and even a young specimen will soon make an impact. Long after the leaves have fallen, the cascade of spreading and weeping shoots makes a pleasing silhouette against the winter sky.

Betula pendula itself, a native of Europe and parts of Northern Asia, can grow to 50 ft. (15 m) or more in a surprisingly short time. Young's weeping birch, however, is a form that lacks a dominant leading stem, which means it grows outward and downward rather than skyward, so it remains compact. It can be grown on its own stem, but needs careful early training to form an upright trunk, so it's usually grafted as a tall standard, when it makes a small mushroom-headed tree.

Betula pendula 'Youngii' makes a great specimen tree set in a lawn, where its shape and cascading branches can be seen to advantage. Its white bark will also become a focal point in winter sunshine.

This weeping birch can also be used effectively toward the back of a bed or border, and is useful for providing a contrast in color, shape, and height.

Spring catkins

Although not especially bold, the small catkins can look attractive in early spring when yellow stamens are prominent on the male catkins. Both male and female catkins, which are produced on the same tree, are nearly always formed in autumn, but it's only in spring that they become a conspicuous feature… a bonus with which to start off the season.

Summer grace

Summer is the time to appreciate the curtains of pale green leaves that clothe the cascading shoots. To see this pleasing birch at its best, give it an open position where the outline can be viewed against an uncluttered background, ideally with some sky behind. Its charm can be lost if planted close to taller trees in the background.

Autumn farewell

Although you won't have the fiery farewell produced by some trees that color well in autumn, this one puts on a more restrained show with the emphasis on shades of yellow that's nevertheless a delightful farewell gift at the end of another season.

Winter bark

The silvery bark, a feature of most birches, is particularly pleasing in winter. In summer it is often partly obscured by the cascading stems.

POSSIBLE PROBLEMS

You're unlikely to encounter problems, but if growing a tree on its own roots (those you buy in garden centers are likely to have been grafted), it may be necessary to tie the young shoot to a vertical support initially until sufficient height has been gained, and to remove some of the lower sideshoots, to produce a suitable trunk.

BUYING TIP

You should have no problem finding this popular tree in garden centers. Look for one with a well-shaped head, with branches evenly distributed around it. Make sure there is no weakness or damage near the graft at the top of the trunk.

Soil

Undemanding, and will grow in almost any soil, but growth may be slow if it's too dry or chalky, and waterlogged soil may cause problems.

Site

Best in full sun in an open position, perhaps in a lawn, but it will tolerate light shade.

Hardiness

Zone 1

Likely height

15 ft. (4.5 m)

plant directory

Betula pendula

Betula pendula is known as the European white birch in the United States. In the UK, it is the silver or common birch. The weeping form is called Young's weeping birch.

Although individual flowers of *Caragana arborescens* 'Pendula' are small, the overall display can be quite bold when the plant is in full flower in spring.

POSSIBLE PROBLEMS

Watch out for suckers arising around the base. These will be from the rootstock onto which the pendulous variety has been grafted, and must be removed.
If the head looks sparse, hard pruning while young may stimulate more shoots and a denser head.

BUYING TIP

The weeping heads are likely to be grafted onto stems 1.5m (5ft) to 8 ft. (2.4 m) high, while other varieties are sometimes grafted onto even shorter stems. Choose one that suits the position you have in mind: although the head may add a little extra height as it fills out, the ultimate height may not be much more than when you buy it. Look for a well-shaped head, with an even cascade of branches all around it.

Caragana arborescens 'Pendula'

KEY FACTS

Soil
This undemanding plant will grow in almost any soil, including alkaline chalky ground.

Site
Prefers full sun but will tolerate some shade. Tolerant of cold and exposed positions.

☼ ☼ ●

Hardiness
Zone 2

Likely height
8 ft. (2.4 m)

This weeping tree is compact enough for the smallest garden— it won't grow to more than about 8 feet—and it's really tough too. It deserves to be grown in small gardens more often.

Caragana arborescens is an upright shrubby plant from Siberia and Mongolia that can grow to 15 ft. (4.5 m) or more, but the variety 'Pendula' has cascading growth and is grafted onto an upright stem of the species. This means you can have a small weeping tree that won't outgrow its space.

It's not showy enough to make an impression in a large garden, but in a small one it will make a pleasing display, especially in mid- or late spring when the yellow flowers appear.

Plant it as a specimen tree in a lawn; or in the ground or in a large tub in a patio area. Much of its impact will be lost if you position it among other trees and shrubs in a border.

The typical pea-like flowers of *Caragana arborescens* 'Pendula.' Once these are over you're left with a mound of feathery-looking foliage.

Spring flowers

The yellow, pea-type flowers in mid-or late spring resemble those of a broom (*Cytisus*), but they are produced less prolifically. Individual flowers grow on thin, downy stalks, usually as the young foliage is almost fully formed.

Summer foliage

The rather feathery-looking foliage is pale green and pleasing even when the flowers have finished. Other weeping varieties are available with narrower leaves, but the effect is the same from a distance.

To make an impression for the summer months, avoid planting against a backdrop of foliage shrubs, or a hedge, which will lessen the impact.

Winter outline

Even in winter this small tree can make a focal point in a small garden if suitably positioned. The bare stiffly pendent branches can look stark yet dramatic when viewed against an appropriate backdrop.

plant directory

Caragana arborescens 'Pendula'

You'll usually find this fairly uncommon tree referred to by its Latin name, but it may sometimes be called the pea tree. This name alludes to the typical pea-type flowers.

Catalpa bignonioides 'Aurea'

Surely one of the finest golden-leaved trees, this is one that stops passers-by in their tracks. The large and bold foliage holds its color well throughout the summer, and there's the bonus of flowers and interesting seed pods on mature specimens.

This beautiful plant is as versatile as it is impressive. It can be grown on a single trunk, or as a multistemmed tree. Sometimes it resembles a large shrub as much as a tree: it all depends on the early training. It's sometimes even grown as a foliage shrub in a mixed border, being cut back hard each year to stimulate new growth from close to ground level (the resulting shoots often have particularly large leaves). As a specimen garden tree, it's best grown on a single trunk when it will make a small tree.

Don't be deterred from planting it if you know the size the green form will eventually grow to; 'Aurea' is smaller and more compact.

Catalpa bignonioides is native of the eastern United States. 'Aurea' is a little more tender than the green form.

Bright foliage

The rich yellow leaves do not become dull or turn greenish as the season progresses (a problem with some trees and shrubs with yellow foliage). The leaves have a disagreeable odor when crushed, but this is unlikely to be a problem if you leave them alone, and it certainly should not deter you from planting this excellent tree.

Bonus flowers

In mid- and late summer, fairly mature plants produce white flowers with yellowish throats, in long upright panicles. These are most likely to be produced where the climate is warm, or when the summer is a hot one. Although not eye-catching from a distance, they are pleasing and worthwhile for close viewing.

Beautiful beans

If the tree has flowered well, and the summer's been a warm one, you may even have a crop of striking seed pods to admire. These look like large bean pods up to 1 ft. (30 cm) or more long, green at first but aging to black. They become a feature in early autumn, and will usually remain hanging into winter, long after the leaves have fallen.

Don't expect your tree to produce a good crop of seed pods for many years, and even then they are more likely to be a feature if you live in a warm area. However, this is primarily a foliage tree, so regard flowers and pods as a bonus when they occur.

Above: In time *Catalpa bignonioides* 'Aurea' can make a substantial tree, but it will take years to reach this size.

Right: The 'bean' pods on *C. bignonioides* and *C. b.* 'Aurea' last into winter. The green trees are usually larger.

POSSIBLE PROBLEMS

In an exposed and windy area the leaves sometimes become damaged and less attractive toward the end of summer. Avoid this by choosing a suitable position initially. If you want a tree with a single clear trunk, remove low-growing branches while young if necessary.

BUYING TIP

If buying in person at a garden center or nursery, and you want a single-stemmed tree, be sure to choose one suitably trained and with a single dominant leading shoot, rather than a shrubby plant with several stems near the base. If ordering by post, make it clear what you want.

Soil

Best in fertile soil, and is unlikely to do well in shallow or impoverished soil.

Site

A sheltered position is better than an exposed one, otherwise the large leaves may be damaged. It's likely to do best in a warm and sheltered position. Partial shade may ensure the yellow leaves do not scorch, but they do grow well in full sun.

Hardiness

Zone 5

Likely height

15 ft. (4.5 m)

plant directory

***Catalpa bignon-ioides* 'Aurea'**

Indian cigar tree is the name most commonly used in the United States, followed by Southern catalpa. In the UK, this tree is known as the Indian bean tree. Other names used include common catalpa, catawba, bean tree, and smoking bean.

Cercis siliquastrum

One of those trees that visitors almost always comment on, *Cercis siliquastrum* has all the qualities needed to make an interesting feature in a small garden. It's almost smothered with bright rose-purple flowers in late spring and early summer, remains small for many years, and usually develops an interesting spreading shape that gives old specimens a special appeal.

This pretty native of the eastern Mediterranean region is a sun-loving tree that does best in warm areas. It's not a good choice for a cold or exposed position.

One of its quirky features is the ability to produce flowers directly from the trunk, or an old branch, as well as the young branches where you'd expect to find them.

It's a good choice where a specimen tree in a lawn is required. Plant with the future in mind: this is a relatively slow-growing tree, sometimes more like a large shrub, which has spreading growth that could be a problem if you put it too close to other trees or shrubs. In a lawn, or given plenty of space, it will be relatively attractive while young, yet still look magnificent and uncramped when it becomes a mature tree.

Masses of flowers

The pea-type flowers are usually rose-purple, but there are varieties with deep purple flowers, and even a white one.

These appear in late spring at about the same time as the new leaves. If the foliage is not well developed at this time, the flowers can give the impression of a rosy-purple mist from a distance.

Interesting pods

Conspicuous flattish seed pods, about 3–4 in. (8-10 cm) long, start to be conspicuous from mid-summer onward. Gray-green at first, they age to a grayish-brown, sometimes with a purplish tinge, and persist into winter.

Autumnal color

Although autumn tints are not as spectacular as the fiery-reds and oranges of some trees, the dying leaves put on a pleasing display in shades of yellow.

Below: The bright pink flowers give *Cercis siliquastrum* an intense color, through this does vary slightly with some varieties. The tree can produce flowers directly from old wood.

Right: *Cercis siliquastrum* is often seen as a multi-stemmed tree, and while young can look like a large shrub. You can also train it as a more upright tree with a single main trunk.

Soil
Requires well-drained soil to do well. Although best on a neutral or acid soil, good specimens can still be grown on chalky soil if it's not too thin. It's unlikely to do well on heavy clay.

Site
Full sun or light shade. It looks best in a lawn or open situation.

Hardiness
Zone 6

Likely height
15 ft. (4.5 m)

plant directory

Cercis siliquastrum

The common name of Judas tree alludes to the legend that it was on one of these trees that Judas went out and hanged himself after the betrayal. Another name, in less common usage, is the love tree.

POSSIBLE PROBLEMS

Slow growth is a common complaint, so don't plant this if you're looking for maximum impact within a few years. It may also fail to thrive and flower reliably in cold areas.

BUYING TIP

You may not find a specimen with a long, clear stem, but don't worry. This plant is more often grown as a multistemmed tree. At first it may look shrub-like, but with age several main trunks will develop from close to the base and form a spreading tree. Container-grown plants are likely to grow away more readily than rootballed plants.

The interesting fruits of *Cornus kousa* are sometimes likened to strawberries from a distance, though they are smaller. Consider them a worthwhile bonus.

Cornus kousa

This delightful multimerit tree has all the qualities you could require: a spectacular display of flowers, fascinating fruits, and superb autumn color... moreover it's unlikely to become so large that it outgrows its space. Consider this choice tree if you want something special and have the patience to wait for your reward.

You will often find this described as a shrub, but given twenty or so years it will become a charming small tree with a bushy habit. Its slow growth means you'll have to wait to see this, but the plus side is that it makes a delightful shrubby plant for a small garden while young.

This choice tree is a native of Japan, Korea, and Central China, and it possesses that special quality that suggests a sense of Oriental beauty. It deserves to be planted more widely, particularly if you can provide conditions in which it will grow quickly and thrive.

Sheets of bracts

What might appear to be flowers from a distance are in fact large white bracts (modified leaves): the true flowers are small and inconspicuous in the center of each set of four bracts. They are borne freely in late spring and early summer, when the spreading branches appear laden with them.

The botanical variety *C. k.* var. *chinensis* is an especially fine form, usually flowering even more prolifically and with larger bracts. It's likely to flower in early summer, the bracts beginning green and maturing to pure white.

Strawberry fruits

In a favorable year strawberry-like fruits may be produced, though not often in anything like the profusion of the flowers. These are edible, but not to be recommended as they are both seedy and bland in taste.

Fiery final fling

In some gardens the autumn leaf colors can be dramatic, in rich shades of bronze and crimson. As with all autumn color, the effect is better in some years than in others.

The autumn color may start early, and linger longer than on most trees... sometimes for as much as a month before the leaves fall.

Cornus kousa flowers prolifically, though the "petals" are actually bracts (modified leaves). This specimen is multistemmed, but the tree is often seen grown with a single trunk.

KEY FACTS

Soil
This is a demanding tree, requiring a deeply cultivated acid or neutral soil to do well. Performance on shallow or chalky soils is usually disappointing.

Site
Best in light shade, but will grow in full sun. Avoid heavy shade.

Hardiness
Zone 5

Likely height
15 ft. (4.5 m)

POSSIBLE PROBLEMS

The most likely complaint is slow growth—don't be surprised if it takes three or four years before you see a flower, and many more before your tree makes a really impressive specimen.

BUYING TIP

You may find this delightful tree in some garden centers, but you're most likely to find it at a specialist tree nursery.

plant directory

Cornus kousa

Although usually referred to by its Latin name, you may find the following common names used: Chinese dogwood, Japanese dogwood, kousa dogwood, or simply kousa.

Cotoneaster 'Hybridus pendulus'

If your garden's really minute or you're looking for a feature for a patio, try this tiny tree. It's really a prostrate shrub grafted on top of a straight stem, so you can be sure it won't grow much taller than when you buy it.

Don't expect a large tree-like plan—it will be more the size of a tall standard rose, though on a mature plant the branches will be more spreading. It's really a prostrate ground-cover shrub, which when grafted to the top of a tall stem of a suitable rootstock forms a weeping standard. Although often recommended for a very small garden, it makes a splendid feature plant for a large garden too, perhaps set in a lawn.

Its main attraction is the bright red berries with which the stems are festooned in autumn, though the small white flowers are an added interest in early summer.

This semievergreen hybrid of garden origin probably has *C. dammeri* as one parent and *C. frigidus* as the other, though *C. salicifolius* may have been involved.

Showers of flowers

Individually the small white flowers are uninspiring, but they are produced in profusion, the drooping stems being studded with them in early summer.

Berry-studded stems

Brilliant sealing-wax-red berries are produced in such profusion in autumn that the trailing stems appear to be weighted down by them. Even better, they normally persist well into winter.

The slightly glossy leaves, about 3 in. (8 cm) long, help to set off the red berries, forming an ideal backdrop .

POSSIBLE PROBLEMS

Fire blight, a disease that can kill the tree, can be a serious problem in some areas. Initial symptoms are wilting of flowers and withering of leaves, followed by die-back of the stems. If detected the tree is best lifted and burnt. Cankers (sunken, rotting depressions on the branches) can also be a serious problem.

BUYING TIP

This popular small tree is widely available at garden centers. The height at which the head has been grafted or budded onto the main stem (usually a species such as *C. bullatus* is used) can vary between about 6 ft. (1.8 m) and 10 ft. (3 m), so look for one that's about the height you want. Be careful if ordering by mail—if you just ask for *C.* 'Hybridus Pendulus' you might end up with a prostrate ground-cover plant. Be sure to order a tree (standard) form.

Soil
Undemanding and will grow well on most soils, though growth may be slow and poor on very shallow chalky ground.

Site
Tolerates sun or shade, but best in full sun. Avoid dense shade.

Hardiness
Zone 5

Likely height
10 ft. (3 m) less if grafted on a shorter stem

Left: *Cotoneaster* 'Hybridus Pendulus' is now considered to be more correctly named *C. salicifolius* 'Pendulus' and is grown mainly for its red fruits.

Above: This cotoneaster forms a small weeping tree when grown as a standard. There are small white flowers in summer and red berries in autumn.

plant directory

Cotoneaster 'Hybridus Pendulus'

No common name is in popular usage.

71

Crataegus laevigata 'Paul's Scarlet'

Don't ignore this neat small tree just because it's tough and easy to grow. These are qualities enough to justify a place on any shortlist, but its neat growth and masses of red double flowers make it one of the finest small trees for late spring color.

This double-flowered red "thorn" originated in 1858 as a mutation on a double pink variety, and it has to be one of the best crataegus for flowers.

You may find it listed as a variety of *C. oxyacantha* (it's been a victim of name-changing by botanists), and synonyms for the varietal name are 'Coccinea Plena' and 'Kermesiana Plena.' The species itself is a native of Europe, including Britain.

Try this tree as a specimen in a lawn: the head is carried well above the ground, the leaves are small, and growth compact enough not to cast too much shade. You'll also find this an easy tree to mow up to and around.

Flower power

The species itself has small white single flowers, but 'Paul's Scarlet' is a much more striking tree with double pinkish-red flowers freely produced in late spring and early summer. 'Rosea Flore Pleno' is similar but pink, while 'Plena' is a white double that ages to pink. All are well worth growing.

Berry bonus

Most crataegus produce plenty of red berries in autumn, but unfortunately you pay a price for the more impressive flowers on these double varieties. Berries may be produced, but they will be scant. If you're looking for autumn interest, consider one of the other crataegus, such as *C. prunifolia*, which is described on pages 74–75.

Crategus laevigata 'Paul's Scarlet' is one of the finest hawthorns to grow for a floral display. It makes a small, neat-looking tree, and although individual flowers are small the overall effect can be stunning.

POSSIBLE PROBLEMS

Suckers sometimes appear from the rootstock around the tree. These should be removed as soon as they are noticed.

BUYING TIP

As these varieties are budded or grafted, so make sure the site of the bud or graft appears strong and undamaged. Look for a neat, symmetrical head.

Soil
**These undemand-
ing plants will
grow in any soil.**

Site
**Best in full sun,
but happy in
partial shade.**

Hardiness
Zone 5

Likely height
15 ft. (4.5 m)

plant directory

***Crataegus laevigata*
'Paul's Scarlet'**

This is one of several
crataegus that share
a number of common
names: hawthorn,
May, quickthorn, and
white thorn are
common ones. More
commonly used in
the United States are
English hawthorn
and quick-set thorn.

73

Crategus prunifolia looks best in autumn, when it's usually laden with red berries. Autumn foliage color is good too, and for a while you may be able to enjoy both at once.

POSSIBLE PROBLEMS

Can be slow to establish, but should eventually grow away more rapidly. Thorns can be a hazard in certain situations. If you don't want low-growing branches making mowing the grass a potentially prickly hazard, remove some of them to give a greater length of clear trunk.

BUYING TIP

Check that the area of the budding or grafting is firm and healthy and does not look weak. Choose a tree with evenly balanced growth.

Crataegus × prunifolia

Soil
**These undemand-
ing plants will
grow in any soil.**

Site
**Best in full sun,
but happy in
partial shade.**

Hardiness
Zone 5

Likely height
15 ft. (4.5 m)

If autumn interest is more important than spring flowers, this is one of the best crataegus to consider. Both berries and autumn foliage tints are impressive, and when you have both together the combination is impressive.

Although it is probably a North American native, the origins of this tree are a little clouded. It may be a hybrid of *C. crus-galli*. Botanists have now determined that it should be named *C. persimilis* 'Prunifolia,' but you may not find this name used by garden centers and nurseries. Provided you look for the word *prunifolia*, you will be planting an outstanding small tree.

It will form a rounded head of branches, sometimes wider than high, and often with branches quite close to the ground. This may make it difficult to mow beneath if planted in a lawn, but it makes a good focal point plant in a grassed area.

The fiercely thorned branches are densely clothed with glossy green leaves, dark above and pale beneath, attractive all summer but superb when they color in autumn.

One of the best hawthorns for berries, *Crategus prunifolia* is usually well clothed even close to the ground. The glossy, dark green leaves turn orange and crimson before they fall.

White flowers

The clusters of white flowers in early summer are not the main reason for growing this tree, though they are a useful bonus. If you want brighter or more impressive flowers, at the expense of a good autumn display, consider the varieties of *Crataegus laevigata* described on pages 72–73.

Beautiful berries

In autumn the bunches of rich red berries are a prominent feature for many weeks. At first they are set off against the green leaves, then these turn into a glowing crimson and the red berries and autumn foliage color combine to create a superb spectacle.

Flaming leaves

In autumn the leaves flare into a blaze of orange and crimson, enhanced by the red berries that make a happy combination.

plant directory

***Crataegus
prunifolia***

This is one of several crataegus that share a number of common names, including hawthorn and May. No generally used common name is applied to this specific tree.

Eucryphia x *nymansensis* 'Nymansay'

There aren't many trees that flower in late summer and early autumn, but this choice plant is one of them... and it's evergreen in the bargain. It can be a demanding plant to establish, but is well worth the effort if you can provide suitable conditions.

You may find this hybrid between two South American species, and some other eucryphias, described and listed as shrubs, but those such as *E. x nymansensis* can make much-branched columnar trees. They are not particularly common as trees, so your eucryphia will probably look rather special. 'Nymansay' is quite fast-growing, which is a further attraction. Unfortunately, it needs a mild and favorable area to do well.

White flowers

The white flowers with yellow stamens resemble Christmas roses (*Helleborus niger*), and look especially good against the backdrop of dark, glossy, evergreen foliage. Usually the tree is covered with them from top to bottom, making it attractive whether viewed close to or from a distance. Individual flowers may be 2 in. (5 cm) or more across.

Evergreen foliage

This is one of a small and select group of trees with large, showy flowers that's also evergreen. This particular tree is a hybrid between two Chilean species, *E. cordifolia* and *E. glutinosa*, and it can be variable, having both compound and simple leaves on the same plant.

POSSIBLE PROBLEMS

It may be necessary to remove dead or winter-damaged shoots in mid-spring. New growth is usually produced to replace it provided you do not live in an especially cold area.

BUYING TIP

Buy a container-grown plant, and put it in during spring rather than autumn. You will probably have to buy it from a specialist tree nursery.

Eucryphia x nymansensis 'Nymansay' can make a beautiful upright tree in time, and is a magnificent sight even from a distance.

The white blooms
of *Eucryphia* x
nymansensis
'Nymansay' resem-
ble those of the
Christmas rose
(*Helleborus niger*),
and are very freely
produced.

Soil

**This is a tree that
thrives best on acid
or neutral, mois-
ture-retentive but
not waterlogged
soil. Alkaline, chalky
soils sometimes
produce acceptable
results, but only if
deeply cultivated.**

Site

**Light or partial
shade is preferable
to a very sunny posi-
tion. It's important
for the roots to be
in shade, even if the
tops are in full sun,
which can often be
achieved by planting
low-growing shrubs
near the base. Avoid
a position prone to
strong winds.**

Hardiness
Zone 7

Likely height
30 ft. (10 m)

plant directory

***Eucryphia x
nymansensis***

Eucryphia x
nymansensis does
not have a popular
common name,
but eucryphias in
general are
occasionally referred
to as brush bush,
while *E. glutinosa*
is sometimes
called nirrhe.

Fagus sylvatica 'Purpurea Pendula'

Anyone who knows how what large and majestic trees purple beech can be, may have doubts about planting one in a small garden! But this weeping form can be planted with confidence, for makes a distinctive small mushroom-shaped bush.

Whether you find this tree attractive or unappealing is a matter of individual taste. It's not a graceful tree like Young's weeping birch (*pages 60–61*), but a rather tight mushroom shape with somewhat angular growth. This means it's very space-saving and compact, and ideal if you want a purple-foliaged tree suitable for a small space.

Use it as a patio or lawn specimen rather than in a mixed border, or among other trees, otherwise its impact will be lost. The dark leaves show up best against a light background such as a lawn.

You may find conflicting advice regarding the eventual height of this tree. Some experts suggest that although slow-growing and remaining small for many years, it will eventually grow large. It may be that there are different forms of the tree, but don't let this deter you—it's unlikely to outgrow its welcome in the timespan most of us plan for.

Purple leaves

The purple-red spring foliage ages to dark bronze-purple, but always retains a strong image. The tightly packed pendulous shoots mean the leaves form a tight purple curtain around the tree, often to ground level.

Mushroom shape

While young the mushroom shape is very attractive, but old specimens tend to become more flat-topped. The weeping growth ensures it's a distinctive tree in summer, and the outline of the bare branches can make an interesting winter feature.

As the leaves fall in winter, the pendulous outline of the branches still adds interest by creating a structured shape that can be a focal point when set in a lawn.

The pendulous branches of *Fagus sylvatica* 'Purpurea Pendula' generally cascade to the ground, and will almost certainly attract attention.

POSSIBLE PROBLEMS

Specific problems are unlikely. If the head seems to be developing unevenly, prune out a few shoots while the tree is still young to create a more balanced shape.

BUYING TIP

You may be able to find this tree at a good garden center, otherwise buy from a specialist tree nursery. Look for a specimen with branches well-spaced around the head.

Soil
Generally unde-
manding, but avoid
heavy clay soil.

Site
Full sun, ideally
in a lawn where
its coloring and
shape can be
appreciated.

Hardiness
Zone 5

Likely height
10–15 ft. (3–4.5 m)

plant directory

Fagus sylvatica

Fagus sylvatica is
popularly known as
European beech;
'Purpurea Pendula'
as weeping purple
beech.

Ilex aquifolium

The ever-popular holly is usually seen as a large shrub, but you can also enjoy it as a fairly large pyramidal tree or a small tree with a clear trunk. They can be clipped to shape and look especially impressive in a formal setting.

There are hundreds of holly species, which have spawned even more hybrids and varieties, but the many attractive varieties of *Ilex aquifolium* are particularly popular. This native to Europe, including Britain, can reach 80 ft. (25 m) if left to its own devices in ideal conditions, but as we all know lots of us grow holly in our small gardens. The best form to consider as a small garden tree is one trained as a standard, with a rounded head at the top of a clear stem. These look especially pleasing in a formal setting, or even in large containers.

Pruning will easily keep your tree within bounds once the head has grown to a size that you find appropriate.

Evergreen leaves

The species itself has green evergreen foliage, but most of the varieties grown in gardens are chosen for their variegated leaves. There are lots of them, with gold or silver the most common variegation.

Typically the leaves are spiny, but some varieties, such as 'J. C. van Tol,' have almost spineless foliage.

Bright berries

Not all varieties produce berries, so make sure you choose an appropriate one, and have a pollinator (*see box "Male or Female?"*)

Typically the long-lasting berries (often still present in spring after a mild winter if the birds haven't been driven to strip them from the tree) are bright red. But even that's not always so, as 'Amber' and 'Bacciflava' ('Fructu Luteo') are among those with yellow berries.

POSSIBLE PROBLEMS

Poor fruiting (or total lack of berries) is a common problem, but the answer's simple (see "Male or Female?" below). Variegated varieties may produce all-green shoots, which should be cut out as soon as they are noticed. This is more likely to happen with varieties that have the color in the center of the leaf with a green edge, than those with the variegation around the edge. If the formative training has not been complete, it may be necessary to shorten long sideshoots at the top by about half to stimulate more branching to form a dense head. If you want a longer trunk, as the tree grows remove some of the lowest shoots back to the trunk.

MALE OR FEMALE?

Unfortunately male and female flowers are often carried on different plants (although some are bisexual). If you have a variety that has all-male flowers you won't get berries. And even if you buy a female variety, you'll need a male plant somewhere nearby to obtain a good crop of berries. You can't judge sex by the name. 'Golden King' is a female, while 'Golden Queen' is male! There are other examples of misleading names. Check with your supplier when you buy. If you want to sex a holly already in your garden, check with a magnifying glass when the small white flowers appear in late spring or early summer. If the flower has four tiny stalks (stamens) in the center, it's a male. If it has one club-headed stalk in the center (the pollen-receiving pistil), it's female.

BUYING TIP

You may have to go to a specialist tree nursery to find a holly trained as a standard or tree form. Hollies do not transplant well, so they should be sold in containers.

Soil

Undemanding and does well on most soils, but best on fertile, moisture-retentive but well-drained ground.

Site

Tolerates sun or shade, but for a well-shaped tree a sunny position is needed to ensure even growth and an attractive shape

Hardiness

Zone 6

Likely height

15 ft. (4.5 m)

plant directory

Ilex aquifolium

Ilex in generally are popularly known as hollies. *I. a.* 'Bacci-flava' ('Fructu Luteo') is called the yellow-fruited holly.

Left: The variegated hollies are most often planted, as they have more year-round interest. This one is *I. aquivolium* 'Argentea Marginata.'

Above: The variety of *I. aquifolium* called 'J C van Tol' is a good choice if prickly holly leaves deter you from growing a holly. These are almost spineless.

Juniperus scopulorum 'Skyrocket'

Choose this distinctive conifer if you want to create tall points and a vertical dimension without taking up too much space. It is an ideal tree whenever you want maximum impact in minimum space.

If you're looking for a narrow columnar conifer, this is one of the very best. The name 'Skyrocket' indicates its apparent desire to reach skyward rather than explore horizontally.

It's a splendid accent plant to punctuate a bed that needs a little height, but a single specimen in a lawn or a fairly flat area can look a little out of place. In that situation it's best to plant a small group of them (at least three and possibly five or more).

You may sometimes find this distinctive conifer sold or listed as a variety of *Juniperus virginiana*. There has been debate amongst botanists over its origins (it was found in the wild as a seedling), but whichever of these North American species it's derived from, you can be sure it's a good choice for a small garden.

Even a young specimen of *Juniperus scopulorum* 'Skyrocket' will make an imposing statement ... while taking up very little space.

Blue-gray foliage

At close quarters the foliage is seen to be made up of small, sharp-pointed scale-like leaves, with awl-shaped juvenile foliage. The overall impression from a distance is of a blue-gray tree.

Pencil-like shape

The narrow columnar habit that gave this conifer its name is what makes it such a useful garden tree.

It's quite a rapid grower, and makes a statement within a few years of planting. Growth slows with age, but even a tall specimen probably won't look out of place because of its small "footprint."

POSSIBLE PROBLEMS

You're unlikely to encounter any problems with this tough plant, once it's established and growing well.

BUYING TIP

You should be able to buy this widely-available conifer at most garden centers. If buying a number of plants to form a group (often an effective way to grow these narrow trees), choose plants that look well-matched in size and shape.

Soil
**Undemanding, and
tolerates chalky
and dry soils well.**

Site
**Best in an open,
sunny position.**

Hardiness
Zone 3

Likely height
15 ft. (4.5 m)

plant directory

***Juniperus
scopulorum***

*Juniperus
scopulorum* is known
as the Rocky Moun-
tain juniper.
J. virginiana is the
Eastern red cedar or
pencil cedar. The
name pencil cedar
is commonly applied
to 'Skyrocket.'

*Juniperus scopulo-
rum* 'Skyrocket' can
be used as a single
specimen focal point
like this, but in a
large garden a group
of three or five often
looks better.

Laburnum x watereri 'Vossii'

Don't dismiss the laburnum just because it's a commonly planted tree. The reason so many gardeners choose it reflects its qualities as a good garden tree: quick growth coupled with a small ultimate size, and a showy display of bright and cheerful flowers.

The widely planted laburnum needs little introduction, as it's such a bright and spectacular sight in late spring and early summer, when its branches are festooned with long drooping chains of yellow flowers.

The only negative thing about the laburnum is its reputation for being poisonous. Although it is a poisonous plant, the only significant danger is if children eat the seeds, which are contained within pea-like pods. 'Vossii' is usually chosen because it produces fewer seeds than most other kinds, but it's also a superior plant anyway with extra-long racemes of flowers, which can reach up to 2 ft. (60 cm).

Laburnum x *watereri* itself is a hybrid between *L. alpinum* and *L. anagyroides*, which though still available are not so widely planted as the hybrids.

Golden chains

A common name sometimes used is golden chain tree, a reference to the long drooping tassel-like racemes that are covered with yellow pea-type flowers in late spring or early summer. The flowers open at about the same time as the leaves, which means that they are not obscured by the foliage.

The flowers are lightly scented, though not everyone realizes this because you have to be very close to the blooms to appreciate the fragrance.

Summer appearance

When seed pods are produced they hang all summer, long after the seeds have been shed. As the mature seed pods are brown, and not particularly attractive, on a small tree they can be cut off.

The branches have upright growth initially, but can become spreading with age. The gray-green trifoliate leaves give the tree a rather dull appearance once the flush of new growth is over, but this is a price worth paying for such a spectacular floral display earlier in the year.

POSSIBLE PROBLEMS

It's best not to plant a laburnum if you have small children because of its poisonous properties. The risk is small, however, so don't worry about planting it otherwise.

BUYING TIP

You'll have no problem finding this popular tree—it's stocked by most garden centers. Some laburnums have a shrub-like habit, where low branches have been left on to produce several main stems. If you want one with a single tall trunk, make sure it has a long and clear main stem with an undamaged leading shoot. If necessary you can remove some of the higher sideshoots later to extend the height of the trunk.

Right: Laburnums respond well to pruning and training, and are sometimes used to form laburnum arches.

Left: It's usually possible to underplant laburnums as they do not cast heavy shade. This one has been been underplanted with alliums, the one opposite with *Stachys byzantina*.

Soil
**Undemanding, and
even grows well on
chalky soils.**

Site
**Best in full sun,
but will tolerate
light shade.**

Hardiness
Zone 6

Likely height
20 ft. (6 m)

plant directory

**Laburnum x
watereri 'Vossii'**

Golden chain and
golden rain tree are
names often used,
for obvious reasons.
L. anagyroides is
sometimes
described as the
common laburnum.

Left: One of the most beautiful varieties of *Magnolia* x *soulangeana* to grow is 'Lennei.' The enormous goblet flowers usually appear in mid and late spring.

Above: *Magnolia* x *soulangeana* 'Amabilis' has ivory-white flowers with just a hint of a purple flush at the base of the inner petals.

Magnolia x soulangeana

Justifiably one of the most widely planted magnolias, this magnificent tree is a real show-stopper in spring when the bare branches are laden with huge and beautiful blooms. Provided it can be given space to spread, this surely has to be on any shortlist.

This hybrid raised in the garden of Soulange-Bodin, at Fromont near Paris, is surely one of the most popular of all flowering trees. It's a hybrid of *M. denudata* fertilized by the pollen of *M. liliiflora* (both Chinese species). It makes a multistemmed spreading tree, and it's the spread as much as height that might limit where you plant it in a small garden. A mature tree can be 30 ft. (10 m) across, though it will take many years to reach this size.

In some ways they are more like large shrubs, and their spreading habit makes them more suitable as a lawn tree rather than cramped in a border.

Many varieties have been raised, varying mainly in flower size and color, though some varieties flower a little later or earlier than others. The normal flowering time is mid-spring, before the leaves emerge, but varieties like 'Lennei' may not bloom until late spring.

Apart from the spelling used above, you are likely to encounter this tree spelt *soulangiana*. The difference simply reflects changing rules of nomenclature.

Beautiful blooms

The crowning glory of this magnificent tree is undoubtedly the profusion of large flowers resembling white tulips stained rose-purple at the base.

Particularly impressive varieties include 'Lennei' (flowers like enormous creamy-white goblets suffused rose-purple), 'Lennei Alba' (ivory white), and 'Rustica Rubra' (pinkish cup-shaped flowers).

Some varieties are pleasantly scented, but flower size, shape, and color are also important qualities.

Autumn leaves, winter buds

There's another brief flush of color in autumn as the leaves turn yellow. Before winter's out the developing flower buds become conspicuous.

Soil
Best on a fertile, loamy soil, and does very well on clay. Not ideal for chalky soils, though they will put on a respectable performance.

Site
Light shade is well tolerated. The tree itself will do well in sun, but the early flowers may be damaged if thawed rapidly by direct early morning sun.

Hardiness
Zone 5

Likely height
25 ft. (8 m)

POSSIBLE PROBLEMS

Often slow to flower, a five-year wait not being unusual. If it doesn't show signs of flowering by then, make sure you are not feeding it too much. Root pruning (severing some of the major roots without damaging the fibrous ones close to the tree) may be enough to induce flowering.
If you don't want a wide-spreading shrubby tree, be prepared to remove some of the lower branches to create a single short main trunk, or to produce a multistemmed tree. Do this in the dormant season.
The flowers are sometimes damaged by frost if they thaw too rapidly after a cold night, resulting in brown petals. Avoiding a position where they are in direct morning sun may help.

BUYING TIP

This magnolia is only rarely offered as a pretrained standard tree with clear trunk. This may not matter if you're prepared to settle for a spreading multi-stemmed tree. Just choose one with balanced growth all around the plant, and an undamaged leading shoot.

plant directory

Magnolia x soulangeana

Sometimes called the saucer magnolia, Chinese magnolia, or tulip magnolia, but usually referred to by its Latin name.

Malus floribunda

A delightful tree when covered with blossom in spring, this ornamental crab apple has all the qualities needed for an exceptionally good small garden tree. And it's just one of many outstanding *Malus* that you could use.

This Japanese tree—some experts consider it to be a hybrid rather than a true wild species—is perhaps the most beautiful of all crab apples when in blossom. The branches are garlanded with flowers in spring, making an outstandingly beautiful sight.

It's a round-headed tree, sometimes spreading with age, and an utterly reliable choice. It's undemanding to grow, flowers while still young, grows reasonably quickly, yet is unlikely to outgrow its space.

Beautiful blossom

This willing tree blossoms in mid- to late spring, the whole tree almost smothered with flowers. Although individual blooms are not large, the overall impact is impressive.

The flowers are rich rose when half open, but fade to pale pink when fully expanded, creating an overall impression of a pale blush when viewed from a distance.

Small fruits

This is not the best choice if you're looking for a *Malus* with a heavy crop of conspicuous crab apples. The round, pale yellow fruit are relatively small at about ¾ in. (18 mm) across.

Blossom time is when *Malus floribunda* makes a real contribution to the garden. The color changes from pink to white, but from a distance the overall impression is of a mass of pale pink blossom.

POSSIBLE PROBLEMS

Prone to the same pests and diseases as cultivated apples, such as mildew, apple scab, and aphids. Unlike ordinary apple trees, it does not require routine pruning.

BUYING TIP

Widely available at garden centers. Look for an attractive and balanced head, and make sure there are no signs of pests or disease.

PURPLE AND RED

Malus x _purpurea_ is similar to _M. floribunda_, but has purplish-red leaves, and red flowers. Its colored foliage makes it a more attractive tree during the summer months. If you want a green-leaved crab apple with red flowers, try _M._ x _atrosanguinea_, which is very like _M. floribunda_ but a richer rose, which does not fade as the flowers mature. There are also many hybrid _Malus_ with attractive blossom and fruits, so it's worth looking at other varieties too.

Malus floribunda is grown mainly for its spring blossoms, but you may have a few crab apples in autumn as a bonus. There are better *Malus* for autumn fruits, however.

Soil
**Undemanding,
provided the soil
does not become
waterlogged.**

Site
**Will tolerate light
shade, but best in
full sun.**

Hardiness
Zone 4

Likely height
20 ft. (6 m)

plant directory

Malus floribunda

The decorative *Malus*
in general are known
as crabs, crab
apples, or flowering
crabs. Purple-leaved
kinds are occasion-
ally referred to as
purple-leaved crab
apples. *M. floribunda*
is sometimes
referred to as the
Japanese flowering
crab apple or showy
crab.

89

It's the fiery autumn foliage colors that make *Malus tschonoskii* special, but it also has a narrow, upright shape that makes it useful if space is at a premium.

Malus tschonoskii

Don't be put off by the name. This tree is a wonderful choice where you need a crab apple with narrow, upright growth... and one of the very best for fiery autumn colors.

This native of Japan can grow tall by the standards of many of the trees included in this book, but its erect, rather columnar growth means it doesn't take up much ground space.

It lacks the flower-power of most crab apples, and the fruit isn't especially noteworthy (brownish-yellow flushed purple, and only sparsely produced), but is a tree to grow for its shape and often brilliant autumn color.

Spring flowers

The late spring white flowers, about 1 in. (2.5 cm) across, are flushed pink at first. Although the blossom is not as freely produced as on say *M. floribunda* (*pages 88–89*), it's nevertheless a showy tree in flower.

Autumn color

Autumn is when this tree excels over most other *Malus*, and its moment of glory is shortly before the leaves fall. The foliage assumes shades of yellow, orange, purple, and scarlet, all the more conspicuous if the tree is fairly tall and standing in a spot where its profile and color can be appreciated, perhaps as a specimen tree in a lawn.

Although *Malus tschonoskii* has pretty spring flowers and small crab apples in autumn, it's really at its best when the foliage turns in the autumn.

KEY FACTS

Soil
Undemanding, provided the soil does not become waterlogged.

Site
Full sun, best seen as a lawn specimen.
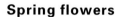

Hardiness
Zone 6

Likely height
30 ft. (10 m)

POSSIBLE PROBLEMS

Prone to most of the same pests and diseases as cultivated apples, such as mildew, apple scab, and aphids. Stem canker can also be troublesome, and usually requires the removal of the affected branch. Unlike ordinary apple trees it does not require routine pruning.

BUYING TIP

Sometimes available at good garden centers; otherwise buy from a specialist tree nursery.

plant directory

Malus tschonoskii

The decorative *Malus* in general are known as crabs, crab apples, or flowering crabs. This particular one is also sometimes known as Tschonoski crab apple, and bonfire tree.

Malus 'John Downie'

This young 'John Downie' gives just a foretaste of the delights to follow over the years.

Wonderful in spring with its blossom, and spectacular in autumn when laden with colorful fruit, this is justifiably one of the most popular ornamental crab apples.

By general consent, this is one of the very finest crab apples for fruiting. Not only does it crop prolifically, but the fruit is among the largest and most colorful of all. Being large the fruit is also popular for making crab apple jelly.

There are other hybrids that hold their berries for much longer (such as 'Golden Hornet'), but 'John Downie' is so showy that one can forgive its more transient display.

This hybrid crab apple has been in cultivation for over 100 years.

Spring flowers

The blossom appears in late spring, pink in bud opening to white. The tree is perhaps not as pretty as *M. floribunda* (*pages 88–89*), but still very attractive when in full bloom.

Colorful fruit

The main reason for growing 'John Downie' is undoubtedly its crab apples: large in comparison with other varieties, rather conical in shape, and a wonderful combination of yellow changing to bright orange and red.

The fruits don't hang very long before beginning to drop. They can make a mess if they overhang a path, and the fallen fruit is best raked up from a lawn. But rather than waste them, pick them just before they fall to make crab apple jelly.

POSSIBLE PROBLEMS

Prone to most of the same pests as cultivated apples, especially mildew and apple scab. Unlike ordinary apple trees, they do not require routine pruning, though it's worth pruning occasionally to maintain an open center to the tree. This will encourage the fruits to ripen and color well.

BUYING TIP

You should be able to find this widely available variety at a good garden center. Buy a tree about 6–10 ft. (2–3 m) high, with evenly distributed branches forming a balanced head.

OTHER ATTRACTIVE FRUITS

If you shop around you'll find many other *Malus* with colorful fruit that are a feature of autumn and even continue into winter. Some of the outstanding varieties to look for are 'Golden Hornet' (yellow), *M.* x *schiedeckeri* 'Red Jade' (long-lasting red fruits on weeping branches), and two varieties of *M.* x *robusta*: 'Red Sentinel' (deep red fruits that hang well into winter) and 'Red Siberian' (red fruits prolifically produced).

Soil
**Undemanding,
provided the soil
does not become
waterlogged.**

Site
**Full sun, best seen
as a lawn specimen.**

Hardiness
Zone 6

Likely height
25 ft. (8 m)

plant directory

Malus
'John Downie'

The decorative *Malus*
in general are known
as crabs, crab
apples, or flowering
crabs. The particular
varieties mentioned
here do not have
specific common
names.

Above: the fruits of
'John Downie' are
larger than most crab
apples and can be
used for culinary
purposes. Be pre-
pared: they do not
hang on the tree for
long.

Right: 'John Downie'
is also a very pleas-
ing blossom tree,
the white flowers
making a lovely
contribution to the
garden in late spring.

Prunus 'Amanogawa'

One of the best Japanese cherries for a small garden, this tree is wonderful in flower, with attractive autumn color and a narrow columnar growth habit that means it doesn't take up much space.

This is one of the many Japanese cherries, evolved in the gardens of that country over two or three centuries, that make excellent small garden trees. It's now difficult to be sure of the species from which they derived, but it matters not a bit in gardening terms: we must just be thankful that they're there.

You might see it described as a variety of *Prunus serrulata*, as this is the species from which most of the Japanese cherries are thought to be descended, but it's more often sold simply as *P.* 'Amanogawa.'

Don't expect cherries too! It does sometimes produce a few small black fruits, but they are insignificant and of no merit.

Semidouble flowers

The pretty shell pink flowers in mid- to late spring have about nine petals, making them semidouble, though some may be single. They're also fragrant, though you need to be close to the tree to appreciate their delicate scent.

Autumn farewell

In spring the young leaves are greenish-bronze, becoming green in summer, then before they fall bidding a bold farewell. Typically the leaves turn shades of orange, yellow and flame, though like the autumn display of most trees the performance varies from year to year.

Columnar growth

Japanese cherries are noted for their beautiful blossom, but this tree is especially distinctive because of its fastigiate (narrow and pillar-like) growth, rather like a Lombardy poplar, though of course it is a much smaller tree.

Even in winter, when the leaves have fallen, the column of upright-growing bare branches can look distinctive and surprisingly attractive against a bright sky.

POSSIBLE PROBLEMS

This Japanese cherry is grafted or budded onto a rootstock from another *Prunus* (such as *P. avium*), close to the ground so that a tree with branches almost from the base is formed. Unfortunately suckers are sometimes produced from the rootstock and should be removed if they are seen. Try to pull them away rather than cutting them off, to reduce the risk of regrowth. In periods where heavy snowfalls are common it may be worth encircling the branches with strong string in several places to reduce the risk of damage being done where they are weighted down.

BUYING TIP

This popular *Prunus* should be readily available at good garden centers. Look for a specimen well clothed with branches along most of the length of the stem. It's normal for this tree to be "feathered" to the base rather than have a clear trunk.

Right: *Prunus* 'Amanogawa' is usually purchased for the beauty of its spring flowers, but in most years there's a bonus in the form of intense autumn foliage color before the leaves fall.

Soil
Undemanding, and will do well on chalky soil. Avoid ground prone to waterlogging.

Site
Full sun.

Hardiness
Zone 7

Likely height
20 ft. (6 m)

Above: The flowers of *P.* 'Amanogawa' are usually semidouble, though some may be single. Though pale pink in color the blossom has lots of impact even from a distance.

Right: The narrow, upright growth of *P.* 'Amanogawa' makes it a particularly useful tree where you want a vertical element without too much spread.

plant directory

Prunus 'Amanogawa'

This is one of a group of *Prunus*, derived mainly from *P. serrulata*, known as Japanese cherries. 'Amanogawa' is sometimes called the upright cherry, Lombardy cherry, or flagpole cherry, all indicating its tall, narrow shape.

Prunus cerasifera 'Pissardii'

This is one of the most effective of the purple trees seen in many small gardens. You can plant it secure in the knowledge that although it grows rapidly when young it's unlikely to outgrow its welcome.

Prunus cerasifera is a shrubby tree native to western Asia and some other areas, but it's the purple-leaved varieties that are popular garden trees. *P. c.* 'Pissardii' (sometimes seen simply as *P. pissardii*) is one of several with dark foliage that are easily confused from a distance. You may sometimes see it listed as 'Atropurpurea.'

'Pissardii,' discovered before 1880 by M. Pissard, gardener to the Shah of Persia, has dark purple leaves. The similar 'Nigra,' a selection from 'Pissardii,' has darker blackish-purple foliage and darker flowers.

The growth is bushy, and the plant can be grown as a hedge, as it will withstand the necessary trimming. As a tree it forms a rounded head, sometimes on a short trunk.

Careful positioning is necessary to get the best from these trees, as the dark foliage means impact is lost if planted with a tall dark hedge, or other trees, in the background. Choose a fairly open position where the tree can be appreciated.

Above: *Prunus cerasifera* 'Nigra' leaves in autumn. There are sublte color changes as autumn approaches.

Right: *Prunus cerasifera* 'Pissardii,' a useful tree for a small garden, although it's best positioned against a light background so that the purple foliage can be seen to advantage.

Spring flowers

One of the earliest trees to flower, in early spring, this has buds that start pink but open to white. They're usually plentifully produced, and open before the leaves, or at about the same time; this early blooming means the flowers are all the more welcome.

The flowers in the similar 'Nigra' open pink, then fade to blush.

Colorful leaves

Young foliage is dark red, but it ages to deep purple. 'Nigra' has blackish-purple mature foliage.

Occasional fruits

This form of plum tree does produce fruits, but not reliably and they are often few in number. They are dark purple to almost black, round, and quite small.

POSSIBLE PROBLEMS

In some areas, especially in rural districts, birds may eat the flower buds and reduce the spring display.

BUYING TIP

You should find this tree widely available at garden centers, but some may be shrubby plants rather than trained as a tree with a clear main stem. If you want a tree on a clear trunk, make sure the young specimen you buy is already well formed. Don't worry if the trunk appears short, as you can always increase the length over the years by removing more of the lower sideshoots as they grow.

Soil
**Undemanding and
will grow well on
most soils, but it's
best to avoid very
impoverished and
dry soils.**

Site
**Best in full sun.
Will tolerate light
shade, but the
leaf color will be
affected by
heavy shade.**

Hardiness
Zone 4

Likely height
20 ft. (6 m)

plant directory

**Prunus cerasifera
'Pissardii'**

Prunus cerasifera is
known as cherry
plum or myrobalan;
'Pissardii' and 'Nigra'
as purple-leaved
plum.

Prunus 'Kanzan'

A particularly popular Japanese cherry, for many this spectacular tree epitomizes the whole group. Laden with spring blossom, and almost brash with its large double pink flowers, it's sure to make a statement in your garden.

Another hybrid raised in Japan many years ago, this has all the classic form of a Japanese cherry. 'Kanzan' (which may also be spelled 'Kwanzan') is a rendering of the ideogram for a Chinese mountain sacred to Buddhists, which gives some indication of its pedigree.

In flower, it's a real eye-catcher, with its rather stiffly ascending branches richly wreathed in blossom. But these features can make it look out of place in an informal or cottage-style garden.

It makes a good "avenue" tree, planted in two long rows that you can walk between, but a single specimen can also look superb if carefully placed. A single specimen is perhaps best used in isolation in a lawn. Its quite large size and distinctive shape generally make it unsuitable for planting in a border.

Spring blossom

The branches are smothered with large, double, dark pink flowers, hanging in bunches, in mid- or late spring. These open purplish-pink but turn paler pink later.

Autumn fling

Although the tree is uninspiring in summer, it puts on another bold display in autumn, when it goes out with a colorful display of autumn color, the leaves turning bronzy-orange before they fall.

Prunus 'Kanzan' is a magnificent flowering cherry that makes a good specimen tree in a lawn. It's almost overwhelming in bloom, but few flowering trees pack as much punch in full flower.

POSSIBLE PROBLEMS

These are not always long-lived trees, and they sometimes die unpredictably. They are prone to diseases such as silver-leaf, and to reduce the risk of infection should not be pruned unless really necessary.

BUYING TIP

Widely available at good garden centers. Look for a well-shaped head and check that there is no sign of damage to the trunk or branches. Large trees do not transplant well, so do not be put off by a small specimen.

KEY FACTS

Soil
Undemanding, but it's best to avoid impoverished or very dry soils.

Site
Tolerates light shade, but best in full sun.

Hardiness
Zone 5

Likely height
25 ft. (8 m)

plant directory

***Prunus* 'Kanzan'**

'Kanzan' belongs to a group popularly known as Japanese cherries or flowering cherries.

Prunus 'Kiku-shidare-zakura'

This is a good choice if you want a Japanese cherry but don't have much space—its weeping growth ensures a bright and bold display on a small tree that won't take up a lot of room.

Perhaps the best weeping cherry for a small garden, this small tree has arching and drooping branches. These are studded with pretty pink flowers in spring, followed by bronze-green young leaves that later become a glossy green.

Although sometimes used as a patio tree, it's probably best planted in a lawn. The cascading pink flowers look superb against the green grass, and the tips of the long cascading branches are less likely to be damaged by contact with a lawn than a hard surface such as paving.

It's worth clarifying the nomenclature, which can be confusing. You may sometimes see this tree labeled 'Cheal's Weeping Cherry,' which is an invalid name. As with many Japanese cherries, you'll also find variations with hyphenation and spellings. You'll sometimes find it without the hyphens, or as 'Kiku-shidare Sakure.'

Flowering curtains

The clear pink flowers hang like curtains on stems that can reach to the ground, a superb sight in mid-spring. They are so full they resemble small chrysanthemums.

POSSIBLE PROBLEMS

Unfortunately this is not a long-lived tree, and it is prone to a number of diseases. Watch out for signs of canker, leaf-curl, and silver leaf disease. Some of these may enter through abrasions where the drooping branches brush against a path or other hard surface. This tree is grafted onto a rootstock, from which suckers may appear. If they do, remove them promptly, pulling them off at source if possible.

BUYING TIP

'Kiku-shidare-zakura' is widely available and you should be able to obtain it from a good garden center. Look for a well-shaped tree with undamaged weeping branches well distributed around the crown.

Prunus 'Kiku-shidare-zakura' is an ideal weeping cherry for a small garden. Its tumbling branches are laden with pretty pink blossom in spring.

KEY FACTS

Soil
Tolerates most soils, but it's best to avoid poor, impoverished ground.

Site
Full sun.

Hardiness
Zone 7

Likely height
15 ft. (4.5 m)

plant directory

Prunus 'Kiku-shidare-zakura'

This is one of a large group of *Prunus* known as Japanese or flowering cherries. It is sometimes called weeping cherry.

Although *Prunus sargentii* may eventually grow too large for a very small garden, it's unlikely to outgrow its welcome in a medium-sized garden for a long time.

Prunus sargentii

Soil
**Undemanding,
but may not
perform well on
very poor and
impoverished soil.**

Site
**Will tolerate shade,
but is best in sun.**

Hardiness
Zone 4

Likely height
30 ft. (10 m)

Here's an outstanding tree that will give you a blossom display in spring and an autumn show that's just as magnificent. It's one of the finest of all trees for autumn color.

Although not such a popular tree for small gardens as most of the other *Prunus* described in this book, this is nevertheless considered by many to be the loveliest of all flowering cherries. It can be quite large, and only barely qualifies for entry in this book on height grounds. While not suitable for a really small garden, it's a good choice where you have a little more space. It's quick-growing initially, then slows down and becomes a fairly flat-topped tree.

In the wild, and in very good conditions in gardens, it can easily exceed the height given below, but not for many years, and in most gardens it will probably remain a tree of modest size. But give it space to develop if possible, so that it makes a well-shaped tree.

This native of Japan, Korea, and the Sakhalin peninsula is reliable and easy to grow, and deserves wider planting in gardens wherever there's space for it.

Most gardeners plant *Prunus sargentii* for its wonderful autumn color, but don't dismiss the spring blossom which, although small, is very attractive.

Spring beauty

Individual flowers are small and single, but borne in such profusion on the bare branches in early or mid-spring that the overall impression packs plenty of punch. The bright pink flowers are often joined by coppery-red emerging leaves, a wonderful combination.

The variety 'Rancho' flowers a little earlier with slightly larger flowers, and a narrower growth habit.

The flowers sometimes lead later to small black cherry-type fruits, but these are not an important feature of the tree.

Autumn color

This is one of the first trees to turn color, usually in early autumn. It also gives a reliable performance, unlike the quality of autumn color of some trees which can depend very much on the season. Dominant colors include orange and crimson.

POSSIBLE PROBLEMS

You are unlikely to encounter any problems with this tough and easy tree.

BUYING TIP

Although stocked by some garden centers, you may have to buy from a specialist tree nursery. Look for a tree with a well-balanced head (these tend to be bushy, branching trees, and a long clear trunk may not be necessary). Bare-root trees transplant well provided they are dormant, but container-grown trees must be used at other times.

plant directory

Prunus sargentii

Although the Latin name is the one usually used, you may come across the name Sargent cherry. Professor Sargent obtained seeds from Japan and helped to introduce the tree into various collections in the 1890s.

Prunus serrula

This tree is well worth growing for its bark alone. It looks so appealing that you'll simply want to keep touching it. It's likely to be a star attraction during the winter months.

A native of China, this distinctive tree is grown primarily for its beautiful bark. It's a small but vigorous tree with narrow, willow-like leaves, and small white flowers in mid-spring. There are much more impressive *Prunus* species to grow for showy flowers, but the outstanding bark is something you'll enjoy for the whole year, not for just a week or two.

It makes a pleasing "avenue" tree, planted in rows that you can walk between, but few small gardens have space for this. The best position in most gardens is as an isolated specimen in a lawn, preferably where its bark can be highlighted by winter sunshine.

Small flowers

The small single flowers, which open toward the end of mid-spring, are white. They are usually produced in clusters of twos and threes at the same time as the new foliage, which means they are sometimes rather concealed by the leaves.

Small, round, cherry-like black fruit is sometimes produced, but is not a feature.

Beautiful bark

Bark may sound boring, but you simply can't pass this tree by without admiring its beautiful trunk. The surface of new bark looks like glistening polished reddish-brown mahogany. Older bark peels, like that of some maples and birches, to reveal the highly polished new bark beneath.

Prunus serrula is a very tactile as well as visual tree. It's difficult to resist touching the tree as you walk past it, and its wonderful bark looks lovely in winter sunshine.

POSSIBLE PROBLEMS

This is not a difficult tree to grow, and you are unlikely to encounter problems with it. You will need patience, however, as the bark is not at its best on young trees. It may take five to ten years before it looks really impressive.

BUYING TIP

You may be lucky and find this tree at a garden center, but you're more likely to have to buy it from a specialist tree nursery. Look for a straight, undamaged trunk. Don't worry about the height of the trunk too much at this stage, as you can remove lower branches later as the tree grows, to produce a longer one.

OTHER BEAUTIFUL BARKS

A number of other *Prunus* species have interesting barks. Among them are *P. maackii* and *P. x schmittii*.

Soil
Undemanding, and will grow well on most soils.

Site
Full sun or light shade, but for maximum visual impact choose a position that receives lots of winter sunshine.

Hardiness
Zone 5

Likely height
25 ft. (8 m)

plant directory

Prunus serrula

Prunus serrula is usually referred to by its Latin name, but you may occasionally find it referred to as peeling bark cherry or birch-bark tree.

Prunus x subhirtella 'Autumnalis'

Trees that flower in winter have to be worth considering. The flowers may be small, but their very presence will cheer you up when all around seems gray and miserable.

This is a tree that comes into its own in the dreary months between late autumn and spring. That's when the small flowers begin to open, often while the autumn foliage is still colorful, and whenever the weather's not too cold and severe you're likely to find a few of them right through till spring.

It's another wonderful tree from Japan, well worth trying to include on your shopping list of highly desirable trees. Be sure to plant it near a path that you use regularly in winter, or where you can see it easily from a window on those cold, dull days.

Autumn color

The leaves usually turn a rich red and bronze before they fall in autumn.

Winter flowers

The small semidouble white flowers, pale pink in bud, are not particularly bold individually, but clustered along the bare branches they make a very welcome sight from late autumn onward. You will usually find at least a few flowers out through until early spring, but they'll be at their most prolific during the milder weather of late autumn and early spring.

Try cutting a few shoots for indoor winter decoration, when you'll really appreciate fresh flowers from the garden.

'Autumnalis Rosea' has pink flowers, while those of 'Fukubana' are rose-madder.

Prunus x *subhirtella* 'Autumnalis' has good autumn color and pretty winter or spring flowers.

Prunus subhirtella
'Pendula,' now more
correctly called *P.
pendula* 'Pendula
rosea' makes a
weeping tree that
flowers in early
spring.

KEY FACTS

Soil
**Will tolerate most
soils well, but
avoid poor and
impoverished soil
or ground prone to
waterlogging.**

Site
**Will grow well in
full sun or light
shade, but is seen
best in a sunny
position, ideally
with a dark
background such
as a hedge behind
to show off the
pale flowers to
advantage.**

Hardiness
Zone 5

Likely height
**20 ft. (6 m)
P.s. 'Pendula Rosea'
15 ft. (4.5 m)**

POSSIBLE PROBLEMS

**You're unlikely to experience any specific problems with this tree, but
it may take five years or more to look substantial and produce a good
display. Even so, it's likely to flower while still young.
Flowering will be affected by very cold weather. Sometimes, however,
if blooming has been inhibited by cold weather during the winter, it
compensates by an extra-special display in early spring.**

BUYING TIP

**You'll probably find this easily enough at good garden centers. Choose
your tree carefully, however, as some are trained as a bushy plant to
make a small shrubby tree. If you want a clear trunk choose one
already growing that way (alternatively form one yourself by trimming
off the lower shoots as the tree grows).**

plant directory

*Prunus x
subhirtella* 'Autum-
nalis'

Known as the
autumn cherry or
winter-flowering
cherry. *P.* x *pendula
var. ascendens* 'Pen-
dula Rosea' is some-
times called the
weeping spring
cherry.

Pyrus salicifolia 'Pendula' is one of those trees that seems to look right in any garden—large or small. It makes a mound of silvery foliage.

POSSIBLE PROBLEMS

You're unlikely to encounter any specific problems, though they sometimes have a poor root system and may suffer in a very dry and impoverished soil. This is best overcome by improving the soil before you plant, incorporating plenty of humus and moisture-retaining material, feeding initially, and mulching if the tree doesn't seem to be growing away quickly. On dry soil, water well until the tree has become established.

BUYING TIP

You should find this popular tree readily at good garden centers. Choose one with an evenly balanced head and branches spaced fairly regularly around the crown.

Pyrus salicifolia 'Pendula'

KEY FACTS

Soil
**Undemanding,
but is unlikely to
do well on poor,
impoverished
ground.**

Site
Full sun.

Hardiness
Zone 4

Likely height
20 ft. (6 m)

One of the best foliage trees for a small garden, this relative of the pear is an outstanding weeping specimen that looks wonderful in a lawn.

It's difficult to appreciate that this is a kind of pear until you look closely in autumn and spot the typical pear-shaped fruits. Its leaves are more willow-like and its weeping habit means that it makes a tumbling mound of growth that trails to the ground.

The species, a native of South East Europe, Asia Minor, and the Caucasus, is a tough tree that seems to look right in most gardens, large or small. Although in time it will grow to the height suggested below, and maybe even a little larger in ideal conditions, it will remain a small tree long enough for most of us not to mind planting it in a garden of modest size.

Although usually planted as a specimen tree in a lawn, it makes a pleasing feature planted toward the back of a shrub or mixed border.

White flowers

The creamy-white flowers, about ¾ in. (18 mm) across, open in mid-spring, set in calyces and flower stalks covered with white "wool." They usually open simultaneously with the leaves, which appear silvery white for the first few weeks, creating a very pleasing picture.

Silvery leaves

Although the narrow, willow-like, leaves open a silvery-white color, they become gray-green. The overall effect when the long, pendulous branches are densely covered with foliage is of a silvery-gray mound.

Distinctive fruit

The pear-shaped fruits, 1–2 in. (2.5–5 cm) long, are hard and of no culinary value. Visually they are an interesting bonus to appreciate at close quarters, but they are barely noticeable from a distance.

Although grown primarily as a foliage plant, *Pryus salicifolia* 'Pendula' has pleasing white flowers in spring... a useful bonus.

plant directory

Pyrus salicifolia 'Pendula'

This tree's common name is weeping willow-leaved pear.

Rhus typhina

This shrubby tree creates a sense of drama, having a flamboyant "presence" that demands attention despite its modest size. Its adaptability and ease of cultivation earn it a place in many gardens.

You're as likely to find *Rhus typhina* described and sold as a large shrub as you are a tree. But whether you grow it as a shrubby, multistemmed tree or on a single stem with a typical tree-shaped head, it will make a statement as a focal point.

This is primarily a foliage tree, grown for its large pinnate leaves, at their most wonderful as they assume their autumnal colors.

Once the leaves have fallen it looks gaunt yet dramatic in its own distinctive way.

A native of eastern North America, this tree can make a spectacular lawn specimen. But unfortunately suckers from the roots are a recurring problem so some gardeners prefer to find a position where these are not so difficult to remove (in a border for instance).

Summer foliage

The leaves often reach 2 ft. (60 cm), divided into pairs of leaflets along their length (pinnate leaves). They are covered with brownish hairs while young, but become smooth by autumn, though the stalks remain downy.

Rhus typhina 'Dissecta' (more widely sold and grown in gardens as 'Laciniata') is a striking female form with deeply cut leaflets that create a more fern-like impression.

Autumn color

In autumn these large and magnificent leaves turn yellow, red, and orange. The whole tree becomes a blaze of color with the vivid, limply hanging leaflets.

Flowers and fruit

Male and female flowers are borne on different plants in late summer. The female flowers form dense pyramids about 4–8 in. (10–20 cm) long. The fruits are also packed closely together in dense upright bristly cones, covered with crimson hairs, which turn brown and are retained into winter.

The male flowers form large green clusters, and lack the appeal of the female form.

POSSIBLE PROBLEMS

The only trouble you are likely to experience is suckers (shoots) coming up from the roots, often several feet away from the tree. You can remove these as a form of propagation and give them to friends, but they can be a nuisance, especially if they come up through a lawn. Remove them by excavating the soil around them and pulling them off rather than cutting, if possible. But wear stout gloves when you grasp them, as many people get an allergic reaction, akin to poison ivy, to this kind of physical contact with the plant.

BUYING TIP

You will find *R. typhina* at most good garden centers, but you may have to buy 'Dissecta' ('Laciniata') from a specialist tree nursery. Usually it's the female form that's sold because the flowers and fruit are attractive features, but if in doubt you can check with the garden center or nursery. If you want a tree grown as a standard rather than a multistemmed form, look for one that has been trained with a clear stem. You can modify the training yourself by pruning out unwanted shoots while the tree is young, but you will still want to avoid one with too many low-growing shoots and no clear leading shoot.

Rhus typhina is grown primarily for its large foliage, which shows fabulous autumn color, but its curious flower heads are a useful bonus. The fruits form bristly cones, which turn brown and are retained into winter.

Soil
Any reasonable garden soil.

Site
Will grow in light shade, but best in full sun.

Hardiness
Zone 3

Likely height
20 ft. (6 m)

plant directory

Rhus typhina

Most *Rhus* are known as sumac, and *R. typhina* is usually called staghorn sumac. Other names sometimes used are velvet sumac and Virginian sumac.

Robinia pseudoacacia 'Frisia'

The golden foliage of this distinctive and unmistakable tree makes it stand out strikingly from everything else, forming an arresting focal point in the summer garden.

Though possibly on the large side for some gardens, this is a tree that you often see planted even in tiny plots, such is the attraction of the golden leaves. Where space is limited, it's surprising how well it can adapt in both size and shape, and still look good.

The species is a native of the eastern United States, but this variety was raised in a Dutch nursery in about 1935. It is now recognized as one of the very finest golden-leaved deciduous trees that can be grown.

Its appeal lies not only in its golden color, but also in the graceful growth habit and sprays of feathery pinnate leaves.

Although it makes a pleasing specimen tree in a lawn, it is an exceptionally good tree to plant toward the back of a shrub or mixed border, or against a dark backdrop, where the bright foliage will shout its presence.

It's also possible to create some wonderful color combinations, such as planting one of the purple-leaved *Cotinus coggygria* in front of it.

Golden treasure

Many trees and shrubs with yellow leaves lose their brightness as the season progresses, and become greener, but 'Frisia' retains its bright golden-yellow through till autumn.

Other attractions

The thorns on young growth are red, though this is not a feature you're likely to notice on an established tree because they will usually be above eye level. Mature trees produce racemes of white pea-type flowers in early or mid-summer, sometimes in abundance, though these are not so conspicuous against the yellow foliage as the green of the species. They are unlikely to be found on young specimens.

POSSIBLE PROBLEMS

The branches have a reputation for being brittle and easily damaged by wind in an exposed situation. It can have invasive roots that have a tendency to seek out drains, so don't plant too near the house.

BUYING TIP

Widely available in garden centers, usually as a standard tree with a clear stem. However, it can also be grown as a shrubby specimen so make sure you choose one suitably trained if you're looking for a traditional tree with a single trunk.

THE MOP-HEAD

If you want a smaller robinia, try *R. p.* 'Umbraculifera,' which is sometimes distributed as 'Inermis.' It's a small, mop-headed tree with a distinctive shape.

Although *Robinia pseudoacacia* 'Frisia' is grown primarily for its golden foliage, a mature tree will have a deeply grooved bark that has its own special appeal.

The pinnate leaves always seem to look bright and fresh. Although they do darken in color toward the autumn, they remain light and bright for most of the summer.

plant directory

Robinia pseudoacacia

Robinia pseudoacacia is known as black locust and false acacia. 'Frisia' is sometimes called the golden acacia.

Salix caprea 'Kilmarnock'

Being exceptionally small, this weeping tree is one that you're sure to be able to find space for. It's at its prettiest in spring, but the weeping shape and small stature make it a pleasing plant all year round.

This charming small weeper is also likely to be found under its synonym of 'Pendula.'

Salix caprea itself is a shrub or small and bushy tree, native to Europe and northwest Asia, including Britain. It's best-known for the very silky catkins produced on bare stems in early spring. The male catkins are the showiest, about 1 in. (2.5 cm) long or a little more; the female catkins grow to almost 2 in. (5 cm), but are not so silky and showy. Nevertheless, they are a popular spring feature.

'Kilmarnock' is a male, though a very similar female form called 'Weeping Sally' (*S. c.* var. *pendula*) is sometimes available.

Silvery catkins

The catkins are silvery when they emerge, due to the silky hairs, but look yellow when fully expanded and open. The period from emerging silvery buds to fully open catkins lasts several weeks and can span early to mid-spring, by which time the leaves are emerging.

Weeping shape

The weeping branches are stiffly pendulous. The outline is quite attractive in winter, but especially pretty when the branches are studded with emerging catkins. When the leaves have fully expanded the foliage forms a delightful green umbrella.

There's surely room in almost every garden for a dwarf weeping tree like *Salix caprea* 'Kilmarnock.' It's at its most attractive in spring, when the catkins are out. The foliage follows a little later.

POSSIBLE PROBLEMS

You are unlikely to encounter any problems with this small and obliging tree.

BUYING TIP

You'll find this tree readily available in most good garden centers. Choose one with a nicely balanced head with the pendulous shoots reasonably evenly spaced all around. There can be confusion over the sex of these trees, so if you're really bothered about the kind of catkins it may be worth checking with your supplier (or going to a specialist tree nursery). However, you'll almost certainly be happy whether you end up with the male or female form, as both are excellent trees for a really limited space.

Soil
Requires fertile, moisture-retentive soil to do well, and is unlikely to thrive on infertile or shallow soils.

Site
Full sun.

Hardiness
Zone 5

Likely height
10 ft. (3 m)

plant directory

***Salix caprea* 'Kilmarnock'**

Common names for *S. caprea* include goat willow, pussy willow, and sallow. The variety 'Kilmarnock' ('Pendula') is generally known as the Kilmarnock willow.

An undemanding tree that
is unlikely to suffer from
significant problems.

BUYING TIP

You will probably have to
buy *S. vilmorinii* and
S. hupehensis var. *obtusa*
from a specialist tree
nursery, but 'Joseph Rock'
is a popular hybrid that's
more readily available in
garden centers.

OTHER
POSSIBILITIES

There are many other superb
Sorbus with attractive and
long-lasting berries; a couple of them are illustrated
below. It's worth considering
some of these if you have
space for a tree that may
grow taller than *S. vilmorinii*.

'Joseph Rock' is a
wonderful *Sorbus* to
grow. It has yellow
berries, and good
autumn color. When
these combine at the
same time,
the result can be
stunning. It's also an
undemanding tree
that's easy to grow.

Sorbus vilmorinii

KEY FACTS

Soil
Undemanding
and will do well
on most soils.

Site
Full sun. Will
tolerate light
shade, but the
foliage and berry
color may not look
so good in autumn.

Hardiness
Zone 6

Likely height
25 ft. (8 m)

Sorbus are popular for their feathery foliage and bright berries in late summer and autumn, and if you're looking for one suitable for a small garden, this is one to try. It's a graceful tree with many merits, and more compact than most species.

This beautiful tree from western China has a restrained elegance that makes it a tasteful rather than brash choice. Its feathery-looking foliage and graceful habit are especially appealing... and it has the advantage of not being as tall as many of the *Sorbus* grown for their berries and autumn color.

It makes a bushy tree or a more upright plant with a typical standard head. Some experts believe that there are two forms in commercial production.

This is a tree to grow among a collection of other trees provided it is not crowded out, or as an isolated specimen in a lawn.

Ferny foliage

The foliage is almost fern-like as it opens, composed of pinnate leaves with lots of small leaflets along their length. During the summer it's a rather dull green, but nevertheless unoppressive and feathery-looking on graceful branches.

Autumn color

In autumn the leaves become tinted with purple and red, a worthwhile display on its own... but even more attractive when studded with the coloring berries as well.

Chameleon berries

Individual berries are small, but held in large and showy, loose drooping clusters. They gradually change color from a glossy red at first, fading through pink to white with a pink flush.

Not only can you enjoy the gradual transitions from one color to another, you will also be able to benefit from berries that persist for longer than those of many other *Sorbus* species. They usually remain hanging decoratively on the naked branches long after the foliage has fallen.

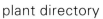

Top: *Sorbus vilmorinii* is worth growing just for its feather foliage, but the berries are fascinating, too. They change from red to white as they age.

Above: *Sorbus hupehensis* var. *obtusa* is another very attractive and desirable tree to grow, this time with pinkish fruits.

plant directory

Sorbus vilmorinii

Although some berrying *Sorbus* are called mountain ash, the ones described here are known by their Latin names.

Ulmus glabra 'Camperdownii'

As this small weeping tree is commonly planted in parks, its familiarity may blind one to its merits as a tree for small gardens. But if you're looking for a small weeping tree to plant in a lawn, this might be just what you need.

Ulmus glabra itself is a large tree that makes an imposing feature in the landscape of its native Europe and northern and western Asia. Don't be put off though, because a lot lies in a name, and if you see 'Camperdownii' added to it you'll know that it's going to make a small tree that you can confidently plant in your front garden even if it's tiny. You might sometimes see it sold or described simply as *Ulmus* 'Camperdownii.' It arose as a seedling at Camperdown House in Dundee, Scotland.

It makes a distinctive focal point as a specimen tree in a lawn, needing to be planted in an open position, in reasonable isolation, for its shape and form to be appreciated.

Mushroom head

The appeal of this weeping tree lies in its mushroom-like shape. The tree is usually top-grafted (grafted at the top of a tall rootstock), and the stems tumble sharply to ground level to produce a mushroom-shaped dome. While it makes an intriguing tree in summer when cloaked in a cloth of green, the bare stems make an attractive feature in winter.

Green curtain

The drooping stems are usually clothed to the ground with green foliage, as though draped with a green tablecloth. The color is light to mid-green, becoming darker as the season progresses. It ends in a flash of yellow before the leaves fall in autumn.

Below: Although elms are usually thought of as large trees, some are perfectly suitable for a small garden. *Ulmus glabra* 'Camperdownii' makes a neat, dome-shaped small tree.

Right: *Ulmus glabra* 'Camperdownii' makes a green dome in the summer, but the tumbling branches are a feature even in winter. This spring shot gives you a good idea of its multi-season attributes.

Soil
**Undemanding and
will grow in almost
any soil.**

Site
**Best in full sun
but will tolerate
light shade.**

Hardiness
Zone 5

Likely height
10 ft. (3 m)

plant directory

***Ulmus glabra*
'Camperdownii'**

Ulmus glabra is
known as the Wych
elm or Scotch elm,
but the variety
'Camperdownii' is
sometimes called
the weeping elm or
Camperdown elm.

POSSIBLE PROBLEMS

**In countries where Dutch elm disease (a fatal fungal disease spread by a bark
beetle) is prevalent, including the United States, the United Kingdom, and
much of Europe, there's a risk of the tree succumbing. Although not as prone
to the disease as some other species, it is still vulnerable.**

BUYING TIP

**In areas where Dutch elm disease is prevalent, you may find this tree
difficult to find in garden centers, but you should be able to obtain it from
specialist tree nurseries. Look for an evenly balanced head with branches
well distributed all around.**

Ulmus minor 'Dampieri Aurea'

A rather narrow, columnar profile and bright golden foliage make this a distinctive tree that once encountered is seldom forgotten. It imprints itself on your memory once you've been captured by its special beauty.

Botanically this distinctive tree is of doubtful origin, and over the years it has been renamed a number of times, but there's no doubt about its garden merit. It's upright shape and golden color make a striking punctuation point in the garden, especially if it's planted among darker trees or toward the back of a shrub border.

You may find it under a range of names, which include *U.* x *hollandica* 'Dampieri Aurea,' *U.* 'Dampieri Aurea,' *U.* x *hollandica* 'Wredei,' *U.* 'Wredei,' and even 'Wredei Aurea.' Given time, botanists may yet reclassify it again! Don't be deterred by this checkered background, for it's a distinctive tree well worth considering except for a very small garden.

The golden leaves of *Ulmus minor* 'Dampieri Aurea' are toothed and densely crowded along the stems.

Golden attributes

This is a tree grown primarily for foliage color, as its tiny pale green flowers in early spring are uninteresting and will probably go unnoticed. The leaves, however, are distinctive and conspicuous: coarse-textured on both surfaces, golden-yellow (a color retained throughout the summer), and crowded close together.

Upright growth

Forming a tight, upright pillar, this is a distinctive tree that looks like a column of gold in summer and has a structural value in winter.

POSSIBLE PROBLEMS

This was once considered to show tolerance to Dutch elm disease, a problem in the United States, the UK, as well as in the Netherlands, and some other parts of the world. Unfortunately it will succumb, so in areas subject to this disease it's a potential problem to bear in mind. However, you may well consider it a risk worth taking for such a striking garden tree.

BUYING TIP

You may find this relatively difficult to obtain in areas where Dutch elm disease has made the various species of *Ulmus* an unpopular choice, and it may not be available at your local garden center. It is, however, available from specialist tree nurseries.

Ulmus minor 'Dampieri Aurea' combines narrow, columnar growth with bright golden foliage that makes it ideal as a focal point tree for a small garden.

Soil
Undemanding and should grow in any soil.

Site
Full sun or light shade.

Hardiness
Zone 5

Likely height
20 ft. (6 m)

plant directory

Ulmus minor 'Dampieri Aurea'

Ulmus in general are known as elms, but the one described here is sometimes referred to as a European field elm or smooth-leafed elm.

glossary. bibliography. index. acknowledgments

Acid soil
See pH.

Alkaline soil
See pH.

Balled-and-burlapped
See Rootballed.

Bare-rooted
Trees dug up from the field shortly before sale or dispatch. These are lifted while dormant, and are usually deciduous. They are normally cheaper for a given size, but should be planted without delay once lifted.

Bush
A rather loose term usually taken to mean a shrub or small tree that's much-branched close to the base, or with a small trunk up to 2 ft. (60 cm) high.

Calyx (plural: calyces)
A cluster of modified leaves that enclose the flower bud. The modified leaves are called sepals.

Chimera, chimaera
A plant derived from the distinct genetic material of more than one plant. This is not merged as in a hybrid, but remains separate in distinct tissue. The tissue of one plant may surround that of another, giving rise to variegation or shoots with different types of growth.

Clone
Stock raised vegetatively by techniques such as budding, grafting, or layering, ensuring the genetic make-up is identical to the original plant.

Collar
In the context of trees, the point where the branch expands in width just before it joins the trunk.

Container-grown
A tree grown by the nursery in a container for most of its life.

Containerized
A term with two distinct meanings: it can be applied to a tree permanently grown in a container, but may be used to describe a tree grown in a field and potted up for sale a relatively short time before being offered.

Crown
The point above which the main branches of a tree grow from the trunk to form a head.

Cultivar
A variety of tree or other plant, raised in cultivation, that is distinct from the species and has been given its own name. It is used to distinguish a "variety" raised in cultivation as opposed to one that occurred naturally in the wild. In this book, variety has been used in its loose sense to include all distinct kinds regardless of their origin. Cultivars are, how-

ever, correctly presented typographically in a roman font with single quotes.

Deciduous
A tree or shrub that sheds its leaves for the winter prior to entering a state of dormancy.

Drawn
Plant with weak, spindly growth, often with loss of coloring, due to lack of light or overcrowding.

Evergreen
Plants which do not shed their leaves in autumn. They appear to retain them permanently, although old leaves are shed slowly over a period.

Graft/grafting
Grafting is a method of propagation, by which a piece of wood (shoot) from the desired plant (the scion) is joined to a rootstock possessing different characteristics. When successful, the tissue from the two plants is permanently fused. Grafting is sometimes used because the rootstock will keep the tree compact, but often it's because it produces plants faster, and more easily, than methods such as cuttings or layers.

Half-standard
See Standard.

Hardy
A hardy tree will tol-

erate frost without permanent damage, although some of borderline hardiness may be damaged without actually being killed by below-freezing temperatures.

Head
In the context of trees, the part growing above the main trunk.

Heel-in
To plant temporarily until time or weather permits permanent planting. The trees are often placed with their roots in a trench with a sloping side, then covered with soil sufficiently to prevent the roots drying out.

Hybrid
A plant derived by cross-fertilization of two species or varieties.

Leggy
A plant drawn upward by lack of light, making it spindly and weak.

Maiden
Usually taken to mean a young tree in the first year after grafting, or after the rooting of a cutting.

Panicle
A branched raceme (see below). A flower head with several branches, which may be opposite or alternate in arrangement.

pH
The scale by which the acidity or alkalin-

ity of soil (and other materials or solutions) is measured. On a scale of 1 to 14, number 7 is neutral; less than this being increasingly acid, greater than 7 being increasingly alkaline. Horticulturally, however, 6.5 is neutral in the sense that it's likely to suit the great majority of plants.

Pinnate
A leaf with rows of leaflets arranged in pairs opposite one another.

Raceme
A flowerhead with individual flowers carried on short stems along an unbranched main stalk.

Rootballed
A tree or shrub lifted from the field with a ball of soil around the roots, and wrapped in burlap or a plastic material (the term balled-and-burlapped is sometimes used). Evergreens, and some deciduous woody plants that do not transplant well bare-rooted, are balled like this.

Rootstock
In the context of trees, the plant on which another variety is grafted or budded.
See Graft/grafting.
The rootstock is usually an inexpensive and easy-to-grow species. In some instances a specific rootstock is used to

impart dwarfness to the tree.

Scion
See Graft/grafting.

Semi-evergreen
Some trees and shrubs are evergreen in mild climates, but may shed some or all of their leaves in a cold winter. Whether or not the leaves fall is likely to depend on where you live.

Shrub
A woody plant with stems branching from near the base, without a distinctive trunk.

Specimen tree
One planted in isolation where other plants surrounding it will not be a distraction, or spoil its shape through competition for light and nutrients. Specimen trees are usually planted in a lawn.

Standard
The term is usually applied to trees with a bare stem or trunk of about 5–6 ft. (1.5–1.8 m) below the head of branches. A half-standard has about 4–5 ft. (1.2–1.4 m) below the head.

Subsoil
The layer of soil beneath the topsoil, usually lacking in nutrients and with an inferior soil structure that lacks humus.
See also Topsoil.

Sucker

glossary

A shoot arising directly from the roots of any plant, or from the base of a grafted plant beneath the graft or scion bud.

Topgrafted/top-worked

A tree budded or grafted near the top of the stem, instead of close to the base, which is more usual. Grafting at the top is especially used for weeping trees if the plant being grafted or budded has a prostrate or strongly cascading growth habit.

Topsoil

The fertile top layer of soil above the subsoil. The depth will vary on the soil type and any rock formation beneath, but the topsoil is likely to be about the top 9–18 in. (23–45 cm) deep. *See also Subsoil.*

Tree

A woody plant; the term is usually taken to mean one with a single trunk and a head that forms some height above the ground. However, some trees produce multiple stems from ground level if so trained while young. Some woody plants can be trained as either trees or shrubs.

Trifoliate

Having leaves with three separate leaflets.

Trunk

The main stem of a tree, between the roots and the head of branches.

Variety

In strict terms, this is taken to mean a botanical variety—a form with distinct characteristics and given a separate name from the one that occurred in the wild. "Cultivar" is a term used to denote a variety raised in cultivation. In this book, however, the term "variety" has been used in its loose sense to mean a particular form of a tree regardless of its origins. However, the correct typographical presentation of the names has been used. *See also Cultivar.*

Whip

A young tree consisting of a single stem with no side shoots.

BEAN, W.J.
Trees and Shrubs Hardy in the British Isles
John Murray, 1981

BLOOM, ADRIAN
Conifers for Your Garden
Floraprint, 1972

BOND, JOHN & RANDALL, LYN
Wisley Handbook: Dwarf and Slow-growing Conifers
Cassell/Royal Horticultural Society, 1987

Botanica's Trees & Shrubs
Laurel Glen, 1999

BRICKELL, C. & ZUK, JUDITH
The American Horticultural Society A–Z Encyclopedia of Garden Plants
DK Publishing, 1997

DAVIS, BRIAN
The Gardener's Illustrated Encyclopedia of Trees & Shrubs
Viking, 1987

GODET, JEAN-DENIS
(translated by Clive King and Helen M. Stevenson)
Mosaik's Trees and Shrubs of Great Britain and Northern Europe
Mosaik Books, 1993

HESSAYON, DR. D.G.
The Tree & Shrub Expert
pbi Publications, 1997

Hillier's Manual of Trees & Shrubs
David & Charles, 1981

JOHNSON, HUGH
The International Book of Trees
Mitchell Beazley Publishers, 1973

LANCASTER, ROY
Trees for Your Garden
Floraprint, 1974

LANCASTER, ROY
Trees for Your Garden
Aidan Ellis Publishing, 1993

MITCHELL, ALAN
The Gardener's Book of Trees
Dent, 1981

MITCHELL, ALAN & COOMBES, ALLEN
The Garden Tree
Weidenfeld & Nicholson, 1998

MITCHELL, A. & JOBLING, J.
Decorative Trees for Country, Town and Garden
HMSO, 1984

PHILLIPS, ROGER
Trees in Britain, Europe and North America
Pan Books, 1978

RUSHFORTH, KEITH
The Hillier Book of Tree Planting & Management
David & Charles, 1987

RUSHFORTH, KEITH
Wisley Handbook: Trees for Small Gardens
Cassell/Royal Horticultural Society, 1987

RUSHFORTH, KEITH
Conifers
Christopher Helm, 1987

SWAIN, BILL
Tree Questions & Answers
Cassell, 1989

The New Royal Horticultural Society Dictionary of Gardening
(editor in chief: Anthony Huxley), 1992

The New Royal Horticultural Society Dictionary Index of Garden Plants
(editor: Mark Grifiths), Macmillan, 1994

The RHS Plant Finder (1998/99) and
The Plant Finder Reference Library (CD-ROM)
The Royal Horticultural Society, 1998
(CD-ROM: Headmain)

The RHS Plant Guides: Garden Trees
Dorling Kindersley, 1996

TOOGOOD, ALAN
Collins Garden Trees Handbook
William Collins, 1990

bibliography

Page numbers in italics refer to illustrations.

index

index

A–Z Botanical Collection/Ron Chapman 40,/Derrick Ditchburn 111,/
Mrs. Ailsa M. Allaby 89,/Mike Vardy 74

Corbis UK Ltd/Kevin Fleming 23

Eric Crichton 17 right

Garden Picture Library/David Askham 22–23,/Brian Carter 18 right,120,
/David England 63,/John Glover 88,/Marijke Heuff 119,/Michael Howes 36–37
/Neil Holmes 59 Bottom,/Jacqui Hurst 50,/Jerry Pavia 69, 81 Bottom,/J. S. Sira
101,/Brigitte Thomas 61, 118,/Didier Willery 62, 90,/Ros Wickham 41 top

John Glover 10–11, 11 right, 11 center, 13 left, 17 left, 17 bottom, 18 left,
20–21, 28, 39, 44 left, 59 center, 60, 76, 83

Octopus Publishing Group Ltd. 49,/Jerry Harpur 48,/Sean Myers 2–3, 4–5,
6–7, 24–25, 30 top, 30 bottom, 31, 32, 33, 34–35, 38–39, 42 bottom, 46–47,
51, 52–53, 54 bottom, 56, 59 top, 64, 65, 68, 71 top, 71 bottom, 81 top, 93 top,
96, 97, 105, 113 top, 113 bottom, 122–123,front cover left, front cover right,
front cover center, front cover background, back cover, front flap, back flap,
front endpaper, back endpaper,/Howard Rice 13 right,/Steve Wooster 27 right

Harpur Garden Library 44–45, 57 bottom, 93 bottom, 95 center, 109

Andrew Lawson 9 top left, 12–13, 15, 19, 26–27, 41 bottom, 55, 57 top,
66–67, 79, 82, 84, 92, 106, 116, 121

S & O Mathews 9 top right, 9 bottom, 10, 11 left, 14, 29, 42 top, 54 top, 66,
75, 99, 107, 108

Peter McHoy 43, 77, 85, 86 bottom, 103, 115, 117 top, 117 bottom

Photos Horticultural 25 right, 78

Harry Smith Collection 73, 91, 95 top, 95 bottom, 102

acknowledgements